VEBLEN
A Play in Three Acts

VEBLEN
A Play in Three Acts

Leonard S. Silk

AUGUSTUS M. KELLEY · *PUBLISHERS*

New York

1966

Library of Congress Catalogue Number 66-20645

PRINTED IN THE UNITED STATES OF AMERICA
by SENTRY PRESS, NEW YORK, N. Y. 10019

TO MARK, ANDY, AND ADAM

PREFACE

Thorstein Veblen is one of the very few economists who have had a significant impact on social thought beyond the boundaries of their own profession. He is probably the only American economist that one can mention in the same company as Smith, Malthus, Mill, Marx, and Keynes.

The purpose of this play is to discover how Veblen came to be what he was and create what he did. As the reader will see, the fundamental explanation offered in the play for Veblen's remarkable creativity was his alienation from American life and the terrific tension he bore within him between a culture that was dying and one being born — a new world whose values he subjected to furious scrutiny.

At the time that I wrote this play, I had been reading a great deal of James Joyce, including his play *Exiles*. Recently I went back to that play and rediscovered this sentence written by Joyce's friend Padraic Colum in the introduction: "To break deliberately with an order one has been brought up in, a social, moral, and spiritual order, and, out of one's own convictions, to endeavor to create a new order, is to embark on a lonely and hazardous enterprise."

And once again — as I was fifteen years ago — I am struck with the close parallel between that remark and Veblen's own explana-

7

tion of "the intellectual pre-eminence of Jews in modern Europe," from which I have quoted in the last act of this play:

> The Jew who searches after learning must go beyond the pale of his own people. But although he finds his own heritage untenable, he does not therefore take over and assimilate the traditions of usage and outlook which the new world has to offer. The idols of his own tribe have crumbled in decay and no longer cumber the ground, but his release from them does not induce him to set up a new line of idols borrowed from an alien tribe.
>
> Intellectually, he is likely to become an alien. Spiritually, he is more likely to remain what he was — for the heartstrings of affection are tied early and they are not readily retied in after life.

Veblen was clearly writing about himself as well — and about all those in literature, art, or science who care deeply enough about their world in all of its complexity — all of its beauty and terror and banality — to achieve a very profound "tolerance for ambiguity," as Herbert Simon has called it. It is this tolerance and this passion that sustain them through the many years required for creative work of the highest order.

❖　❖　❖

The reader may be curious as to how this play came to be written. In 1951 I was a Fulbright Scholar in Norway and felt cut off from my own country, bored with the research study I had set out to do, and restless for something that would engage my energies. A fellow Fulbrighter — a theater director — wanted to do a play and asked me to try my hand at one. By the time my play was done, this Fulbrighter had disappeared from my life. So I took the play to Hans Jacob Nielsen, the director of the Norwegian People's Theater, who liked it and bought it for production in his theater. He had it translated into Norwegian — but, alas, Nielsen died before *Veblen* was ever produced. Meanwhile, I had gone off to Paris to become Assistant Economic Commissioner in a great bureaucracy known as the United States Mission to the North Atlantic Treaty Organization and Other European Regional Organizations (USRO). It would be a lie to say that I forgot about the play completely after that. But the manuscript went into one of a number of cardboard cartons, along with all the other junk of my life that I intend to look at again some day.

Then, last spring, a mutual friend of Augustus Kelley's and mine happened to sit next to me at a banquet of economists. I asked after Mr. Kelley's well-being and learned that he was prospering, having become Veblen's principal (almost exclusive) publisher in this country. I expressed my delight over this news and said that I was an old Veblen buff myself — and had even once written a play about him.

In due course Gus Kelley called me and asked to see the play. And that is how it came to be exhumed from my cardboard midden.

✿   ✿   ✿

All I knew about Veblen's life when I wrote this play came from Joseph Dorfman's splendid *Thorstein Veblen and His America*. I tried to be as faithful as I could to Dorfman's account, but of course every man's life is subject to widely-varying interpretations (including several of his own). I have no idea whether I have got Veblen down right. I was much encouraged to think that I had, however, by a conversation I had a few weeks ago with Professor Emeritus Leland Hazard of the Carnegie Institute of Technology, during the last few hours of my tenure there as Ford Foundation Visiting Research Professor. Mr. Hazard had been a student of Veblen's at the University of Missouri. Indeed, Hazard turns up (anonymously) as a character in my own play. He is obviously the third boy in the classroom scene in Act III.

In an autobiography that he is writing, Hazard relates that, at the last class session, Veblen asked him to stop at his desk. "Will you be coming to class next Tuesday?" Veblen asked. Hazard said yes, he would, because it was the day set for the final examination. Veblen said, "Yes, and if you will put these questions on the board, I shall not need to come," and handed Hazard an unsealed envelope. Hazard recalls:

> It was well-known that he gave everyone a medium grade, M, doubtless because he never read the examination papers.

He gave me the next best grade, an S, probably because he did not have to come to class — in any case not because I had opened the envelope.

But, as in everything else, Veblen had a theory for what he was doing; as I was able to remind Lee Hazard, Veblen had explained his peculiar grading system — in *The Theory of Business Enterprise:*

> There is . . . a large resort to business methods in the conduct of the schools; with the result that a system of scholastic accountancy is enforced both as regards the work of the teachers and the progress of the pupils; whence follows a mechanical routine, with mechanical tests of competency in all directions. This lowers the value of the instruction for purposes of intellectual initiative and a reasoned grasp of the subject-matter. This class of erudition is rather a hindrance than a help to habits of thinking. It conduces to conviction rather than to inquiry, and is therefore a conservative factor.

Whatever one may think of Veblen's grading system, lecturing performances, economic doctrines, literary style, or lack of conformity to the sexual mores of college campuses of his time, the fact is that the man produced a batch of students — including Leland Hazard, Wesley C. Mitchell, Isador Lubin, Walter W. Stewart, Walton Hamilton, Leon Ardzrooni, Leo Wolman, William and R. L. Duffus, to name a few — of whom any teacher might be proud. These turned out to be very different types of individuals who did not necessarily share their teacher's social values or conclusions, though they all revered him as a teacher. Somehow they learned from him to care, to be skeptical, to be bold, to think for oneself, and to struggle to make something new and useful.

Veblen's influence can, I think, still be fruitful for anyone who wants to tackle important tasks in any field. One must learn the cost of major intellectual or artistic endeavor. For Veblen himself, this cost was heavy. He ended his career apparently convinced that he had failed miserably.

Leonard Silk

Montclair, New Jersey
January 29, 1966

CHARACTERS

THORSTEIN VEBLEN

THOMAS ANDERSON VEBLEN, his father

KARI THORSTEINSDATTER VEBLEN, his mother

ANDREW, his brother

EMILY, his sister

ELLEN ROLFE

PRESIDENT NOAH PORTER

PROFESSOR J. LAWRENCE LAUGHLIN

PROFESSOR LASSITER

ASSOCIATE PROFESSOR THAYER

ASSISTANT PROFESSOR BALDWIN

PRESIDENT PORTER'S SECRETARY

STUDENTS

PROLOGUE

Faribault, Minnesota, September, 1874

The seventeen-year-old Veblen leans against the wall of a general store. He is tall, gaunt, and toughly built; he wears a coat of calf-skins, and calf-skin shoes, home made. He is whittling at a block of wood. Two town boys swagger down the plank walk, see Veblen, stop.

FIRST BOY

[*Pinching his nose.*]

I can smell it from here.

SECOND BOY

Sure it ain't the manure pile?

FIRST BOY

What's the difference?

[*They laugh*]

Enter two girls from the right. They are dressed in fancy town clothes — lace shirtwaists, full skirts, bustles, French shoes, feathered hats. The girls mince past Veblen and enter the store. Veblen follows them with his eyes. The other boys notice this.

FIRST BOY

Look at the bastard!

SECOND BOY

Hey, Norskie, what you looking at?

VEBLEN

[*Putting his knife away.*] Oh, dry up!

FIRST BOY

[*Crossing to* VEBLEN, *with second boy following.*] Dry up! It speaks English.

SECOND BOY

Who said Norwegian Indians was allowed to speak a white man's language?

VEBLEN

I'll speak any language I feel like.

FIRST BOY

Ain't we smart? Listen, you dirty Scandihoofian, you better watch yourself. I got my eye on you.

VEBLEN

See much?

FIRST BOY

Too much. Too much of your ugly Norskie face. You get the hell out of this town. You stay the hell back on the farm with the rest of the pigs!

SECOND BOY

[*Roars.*] That's a good one! With the rest of the pigs!

VEBLEN

I'll go where I like. It's a free country.

FIRST BOY

I'll free country you, you lousy squarehead.

VEBLEN

Don't call me that.

FIRST BOY

[*Shoving his face up to* VEBLEN's.] Dirty Norwegian Indian, I seen you! You keep your dirty Norskie eyes off them girls.

[*While first boy is talking, second boy circles around behind* VEBLEN.]

VEBLEN

I'll look where I like.

FIRST BOY

Stick to your country sluts. You ain't fit to look at a decent girl.

VEBLEN

I'll do what I want.

FIRST BOY

You'll get the hell outa this town, that's what you'll do.

VEBLEN

Who's gonna make me?

FIRST BOY

I am, Yellow-Belly!

VEBLEN

Let's see you try, Ass-Face!

FIRST BOY

You'll see plenty, Yellow-Belly!

VEBLEN

Who's afraid of you, Ass-Face?

FIRST BOY

You are, Yellow-Belly.

[*The second boy has stealthily crouched down behind* VEBLEN. *The first boy suddenly pushes* VEBLEN *backward; he falls over the second boy. The town boys roar.* VEBLEN *slowly picks himself up. The second boy, mocking* VEBLEN, *stays on the ground, imitating a pig.*]

SECOND BOY

I'm a Norskie! Oink! Oink.

FIRST BOY

[*Making a fist.*] You want some more?

VEBLEN

Sure.

[*Suddenly* VEBLEN *swings on the boy on the ground, and kicks him with full force in the head — the boy sprawls unconscious. The first boy lunges at* VEBLEN. VEBLEN *grabs him, catches his flailing fist, twists his arm behind him, and forces the boy down to the ground.*]

VEBLEN

Say you'll stop!

FIRST BOY

Go to hell, Norskie!

VEBLEN

[*Twisting the boy's arm, shoving his face into the ground.*] Say you'll stop! Say you'll stop!

> [*The boy says nothing. With* VEBLEN *holding the boy down, twisting his arm, the lights come up on Scene 1, set downstage. During the first minute of Scene 1, the lights upstage, stay on* VEBLEN *and the town boys, one sprawled out, the other struggling and grunting under* VEBLEN. *Slowly the scene upstage in front of the general store fades out . . .*]

ACT I

Kitchen of the Veblen farm in Wheeling Township, Minnesota. Settles, carved tables, chairs, household implements, etc. The mother, Kari, her sleeves rolled up, her arms white with flour, stands kneading dough. She is in her middle forties; her figure is sturdy but womanly. Her speech comes from her deep, vibrant, and singing.

Her daughter, Emily, a slim, pretty girl of sixteen, is ironing. Emily's speech is nervous and shrill.

It is nine o'clock in the evening.

EMILY

The part *I* can never understand is why the captain dumped you in Hamburg.

KARI

If you could see him, you'd know why. A sea-captain! A sea-captain with a face like a banker, fat and tight. A face like a balloon!

EMILY

But why, Mother, *why?*

KARI

"Why?" my two-year-old asks. For the money! Money, maybe you have heard of money? He had our money, why should he want us? To eat his salt-pork? To use his cargo space?

EMILY

Well, I'm sorry, Mother. How can I understand if . . .

21

KARI

If you'd been there, you would understand something. You should only know what your parents went through. The crying! The swearing! A lot of good it did us. We were stuck, but we had to get to America. Your father worked on the docks and kept his eyes open for a ship that would take us cheap. I washed clothes in a laundry. Fourteen hours a day for a month! Finally a square-rigger from Bergen sailed into Hamburg. Your father went aboard to talk to the skipper, but he would take no passengers. Your father begged him, and at last he agreed. He took us and the Hansens and the Bangs and the Kroghs and the Warbergs. Ten grown-ups and twelve children. Thank God we had no children then! You're listening to me, Emily? This I want you to hear! You're old enough to know something!

EMILY

[*Resisting.*] Mother . . . please . . .

KARI

Every child died! Every child and Herr Krogh and Fru Bang! Your father fell sick from the fever and so did I. When we came to Ellis Island, we had train fare to Milwaukee and nothing more. Half-dead we came to Milwaukee, five months after we sailed from Drammen. Sick and alone in a rooming-house in Milwaukee. "Tonight I rest," your father said, "and tomorrow I work." "You are crazy," I said. "You will kill yourself." But in the morning he got up and walked twenty-eight miles to Port Washington and got a job in Stephen Olson's fanning-mill. He had left me all the money we had, a dollar and eighty-five cents. For three days I heard nothing. Then a letter came, and I walked to Port Washington, and Olson gave me a job in the mill, sweeping up. Two weeks we worked in the mill and then we could work no more. Too sick. Almost dead. You know who saved us?

EMILY

Stephen Olson. I know.

KARI

Yes, Stephen Olson, God bless him. He saved us. He and poor Fru Olson, God rest her soul . . . Now you see? Is it any wonder we love our own people? The Yankees would have let us die . . . I could tell you plenty of other times. Plenty! So we learned to stick together! So learn something from your parents! I only hope you don't have to learn it for yourself!

EMILY

[*Trying to break in.*] Mother, I know . . .

KARI

You still don't know what I'm trying to tell you! Emily, I've got good reasons for what I'm telling you.

EMILY

Mother, don't holler at me, but . . .

KARI

When your father gets home, maybe you'll see why. [*Notices* EMILY's *hurt silence.*] So? Talk, Emily — if you have something to say.

EMILY

Mother, you can't expect it all to mean the same thing to us as it means to you. [*Stops.*]

KARI

Well? Go on!

EMILY

To you only Norwegians are good. Everybody else is rotten.

KARI

You stay with your own kind. Yes!

EMILY

To you Norway is the center of the world. To me it is — a word, a word you say, a word in the newspaper —

KARI

It is home!

EMILY

So it is home. But it's not . . . Mother, *you* must try to understand, too . . . understand how it feels to have a home that is — a word, a word I hear and hear and can't understand!

KARI

Your brother Andrew understands!

EMILY

And my brother Thorstein doesn't. You can't make us all the same.

KARI

You and Thorstein! Two fools!

EMILY

[*Putting the ironed clothes away.*] Mother, don't make it a fight every time I don't agree with you. It's just a discussion.

KARI

Well, who's fighting? I'm discussing it! . . . Emily, is that a place for the iron? Put it where it belongs!

EMILY

I should know better by now!

KARI

I'm sorry you have such a hard mother. But I am too old to learn from you, so you learn something from me.

EMILY

All right, Mother.

KARI

I know it doesn't mean anything to you. But it better before you learn it yourself the way we did.

EMILY

Oh, what's the use?
[*The door opens, and* THOMAS ANDERSON VEBLEN *enters. He is a tall, slow-moving man.* KARI *upset by her conversation with* EMILY, *stares at him fixedly.* EMILY *runs to help him out of his overcoat.*]

THOMAS

This is my greeting, Kari?

KARI

I'm sorry. You gave me a start. I didn't hear the horse.

THOMAS

And why should you hear the horse? Did you think I would be galloping all the way from Northfield, in a frenzy to be home after a week?

KARI

To me it seems longer.

THOMAS

Ah, that is more like it.

EMILY

How is Andrew, Father?

THOMAS

How should Andrew be? The same as a week ago: talkative, pious and healthy.

KARI

Never mind. I wish Thorstein had what Andrew has.

THOMAS

Thorstein has something else. Be grateful . . .

KARI

All I ask for my children is that they stay out of jail.

THOMAS

I ask much more.

KARI

Maybe you ask too much.

EMILY

What shall *I* become, Father? A writer? A poet?

THOMAS

Why not? You come from a nation of story-tellers.

KARI

And from a family of farmers.

THOMAS

You'll become what you can. That is all I ask: that you try, that you work!

EMILY

[*Looking first at* KARI, *then to him.*] Well, I *do* try, Father . . .

THOMAS

I know you do . . . Now, girl, you had better run along to bed. I have something to talk over with your mother.

EMILY

Oh, Father, I'm a big girl!

THOMAS

If you were little, you could stay.

EMILY

Tell me the secret tomorrow?

THOMAS

Sure thing. Good night!

EMILY

Good night, Father: good night, Mother. [*Exit.*]

KARI

So you *haven't* changed your mind?

THOMAS

No. On this I will never change my mind.

KARI

You have built the shack?

THOMAS

It's not a shack. It's a house. The work went fast. Andrew helped me, and it's done in a week.

KARI

Craziest thing you have ever done. What will the neighbors say?

THOMAS

Same as you, no doubt. No, worse — crazy, they'll say, and blasphemous, disloyal, anti-Norwegian, anti-Lutheran, stuck-up and pig-headed. Anything else?

KARI

They all think it was bad enough to send Andrew to college. When they hear you mean to ship Thorstein and Emily there, they'll be sure you've gone out of your mind.

THOMAS

I can't help that. They *are* going.

KARI

If you had to do it, why Carleton, a Yankee school? Luther, a school built by our own people, isn't good enough for them?

THOMAS

They live in America, let them be Americans . . . Where is Thorstein — sleeping?

KARI

Don't be funny! He hasn't been home since dinner. Thomas, I am worried about that boy. He doesn't seem to know whether he eats or sleeps or stands on his head. Such a wild one!

THOMAS

Like his father?

KARI

Worse! I never know where to find him. He disappears, and maybe he's up in the loft, lying with his feet in the air and his neck on the floor, reading, or maybe he's deviling the girls over at Halvorsen's or Moe's, or maybe he's fighting in the schoolyard or taking apart the platform binder . . . The neighbors say he's odd . . .

THOMAS

He's not odd. He just doesn't know what he's here for . . . It's a common disease at his age. I had it myself. You remember how they used to talk about me when I wouldn't stay in Valders, when I wandered down to Christiania, and over to Bergen. A boy wants to get hold of the world, Kari, wrap his hands around it . . .

KARI

But he's wild! He won't work. They'll send him home!

THOMAS

He will work. For himself and because he knows what it means to me.

KARI

Knows what it means to you! He doesn't even know he's going!

THOMAS

Kari, I know him better than you do. I am not going to argue with him, I am not going to explain. Tomorrow I'm telling him to get into the buggy with his sister and we are driving to Northfield, and they are staying there in the house I have built. Their food and clothing they will have from home. The cash for books and tuition we can afford.

KARI

We can?

THOMAS

I hope we can. We'll manage.

KARI

So you've got it all figured out . . . Even our daughter . . . Who ever heard . . .

THOMAS

She's as good as anyone . . . And when Andrew graduates, I don't want Thorstein to have the house to himself. He's too fond of the girls . . . I don't want him to get kicked out of that school.

KARI

And if he doesn't get kicked out — what then?

THOMAS

Then will be time enough . . . Thorstein could make a preacher . . .

KARI

A preacher! Don't make me laugh!

THOMAS

[*At the window.*] The boy's outside. You better get his and Emily's things ready for the morning.

[KARI *starts putting the pans of dough away to rise overnight. Enter* THORSTEIN VEBLEN. *His face has a smear of mud down one side of it, his left eye is swelling, and his hands are filthy. He is limping slightly.*]

THORSTEIN

Father, you're back! Welcome home!

THOMAS

[*Ironically.*] The same to you.

THORSTEIN

Greetings, Mother!
[KARI *says nothing: gives him a hard look.*]

THORSTEIN

Do I get the silent treatment?

KARI

I'll silent treatment you! If you think you're too big for me to take a switch to, you're mistaken.

THORSTEIN

Don't you even want to know what happened?

KARI

A cow sat on you?

THORSTEIN

I was in a fight.

THOMAS

Get licked?

THORSTEIN

By no means, Father! Have faith in your son. He knocked hell out of two of them.

THOMAS

Two of whom?

THORSTEIN

Two of those stinking Yankees.

THOMAS

Son, don't use insulting language about another race.

THORSTEIN

They ain't another race, and, besides, that was exactly it. That's what started it.

KARI

What started what?

THORSTEIN

That overgrown redhead, the one I call Ass-Face . . .

KARI

Thorstein!

THORSTEIN

Well, that's what I call him. Anyway, he called me a Norwegian Indian. So I let him have it. And his crony jumped me. I beat the two of them.

THOMAS

You found it offensive to be described as a Norwegian Indian?

THORSTEIN

Well, I thought probably the Indians wouldn't like it.

THOMAS

I see. And just what did you do to make them call you a Norwegian Indian?

THORSTEIN

Nothing. I was just hanging around Robinson's store . . .

KARI

Watching the skirts?

THORSTEIN

Sure, watching the skirts . . .

THOMAS

See much?

THORSTEIN

With those corsets they wear! Should say not! They walk like this [*imitates them*] — like they were being strangled to death by a python. Can't see why the silly fools wear them!

THOMAS

That's why. To get hobbled. To be unfit for work.

KARI

All those Yankee women are good for is to dress up and worry about their nerves.

THOMAS

True. But why, Kari? *Why* are they so useless?

KARI

What kind of question is that? They're useless because they're useless.

THOMAS

No, they are useless to show they are better than a low-class woman like yourself, who *must* work! Their men want them that way: expensive and useless. So they wear bonnets that make it impossible to bend over, French heels that make it impossible to walk, skirts that make it impossible to turn around or climb a fence or milk a cow, corsets . . .

THORSTEIN

. . . corsets that a cannonball couldn't penetrate!

THOMAS

Let alone *you,* son!

KARI

You listen to me, Thorstein Veblen. When the time comes, you marry a nice Norwegian girl that can have kids and keep a house clean and not put on airs. Good night! [*Leaving.*] You coming, Thomas?

THOMAS

I'll be along in a few minutes, Kari. [*Exit* KARI. THOMAS *walks across the room, his back to* THORSTEIN. *Then* THOMAS *turns to him.*] THORSTEIN, why do you hang around that town so much?

THORSTEIN

I don't know . . . It interests me.

THOMAS

Do you like it?

THORSTEIN

No . . . If anything, I hate it.

THOMAS

But do you want it?

THORSTEIN

No, not the town. Not that. Something else.

THOMAS

You look out for that town. The people there will buy you and they'll sell you, if they can. Once they bought me and sold me. Now they can't touch me.

THORSTEIN

Not much they can't. You going to build a moat around this castle?

THOMAS

I don't want them to touch *you!*

THORSTEIN

How're you going to stop them? They touched me tonight . . . And I touched them back! They won't forget it for a while.

THOMAS

Don't be so proud of yourself just because you can fight a little.

THORSTEIN

You wanted me to lie down?

THOMAS

No. If they go after you, you've got to fight them. But don't take
any pleasure in it. That's something for lords and dukes and other
useless beings to take pride in . . . You be proud if you can tell the
truth.

THORSTEIN

Tell the truth about what?

THOMAS

Anything, everything. Your family, this country, this world . . .
yourself.

THORSTEIN

I don't want to . . . I mean, about myself. The rest is all right.

THOMAS

You've got nothing to be ashamed of.

THORSTEIN

I feel as if I have.

THOMAS

What? What have you done?

THORSTEIN

Oh, nothing. Nothing like that. I just don't like them laughing
at me.

THOMAS

Let them laugh. You'll show them. You showed 'em tonight.

THORSTEIN

And you said fighting was nothing.

THOMAS

I'm afraid you'll have plenty more of it.

THORSTEIN

Why don't they just leave me alone?

THOMAS

Not you, boy. Us.

THORSTEIN

All right, why?

THOMAS

Because they're ignorant. Because they're members of a tribe, and they figure we are members of another tribe, so they are afraid of us and dislike us and think we're peculiar . . . So they laugh at us to try to hurt us.

THORSTEIN

They succeed.

THOMAS

[*Going to him.*] It won't last forever, son. They'll get tired of it.

THORSTEIN

Never.

THOMAS

You'll see. [*Puts arms around him.*] Come on, boy, wash up and turn in. You've got a big day ahead of you tomorrow.

THORSTEIN

What's happening tomorrow?

THOMAS

God knows.

THORSTEIN

Does he?

THOMAS

So they say . . . Wash yourself clean! [*Exit*]

Scene 2

The lights close in on Thorstein, washing . . . The lights widen again on a half-sized stage. It is now the main room of the small house at Carleton College, Northfield, Minnesota, that Thomas Veblen built for his children. Home-made furniture, books in packing cases, a bed in one corner, a sink, cooking utensils, etc.

It is a Sunday in June, 1880. Emily, now twenty-two and good-looking, is fixing a kettle of tea on the stove. Andrew Veblen, twenty-six, tall, wearing stiff collar and black tie, a suit slightly too small for him, celluloid cuffs, is sitting at a writing table, books and paper in front of him. Thorstein, now twenty-three, is at the sink, washing . . . making quite a job of it.

EMILY

You're going to wash the skin right off your face!

THORSTEIN

[*Soap in his eye.*] Give me the towel!

EMILY

Here, foolish! You'll shine so she won't recognize you.

THORSTEIN

All of a sudden I have to make apologies for washing myself.

EMILY

Oh, you're a great actor!

THORSTEIN

I don't even think she's coming. It wasn't that definite.

EMILY

Not coming!

THORSTEIN

I didn't say she *wasn't*. I only said . . .

EMILY

I heard you. Simply looking for an out in case she doesn't.

THORSTEIN

You're so clever! A lot you know . . .

EMILY

What exactly did she say?

THORSTEIN

She said she'd *like* to come.

EMILY

How very Delphic of her!

ANDREW

[*Looking up from his books.*] What's so mysterious? "Like to" means "yes".

THORSTEIN

Ah, the House Logician has reported. "Like to" means "yes"! . . .
You don't know Ellen.

EMILY

Maybe she can't make it. This *is* Sunday.

ANDREW

"All Sabbath and evening association between the sexes is for-
bidden," saith the Manual, "except by special permission . . ."

THORSTEIN

. . . of the copyright owner. Ellen Rolfe owns the copyright.
Her uncle John — don't you forget it! — is our beloved President
Strong.

EMILY

She does about as she pleases, Andrew. The *mater dolorosa* is
afraid to touch her.

THORSTEIN

I'm not afraid to.

EMILY

I wish you were.

THORSTEIN

Sometimes I am.

EMILY

Not often enough . . . Are you going to say anything to Mother
and Father about her?

THORSTEIN

There . . . there isn't that much to tell. I don't know — I'll decide
when they get here. Unless Ellen decides for me sooner.

EMILY

Don't you know your own mind?

THORSTEIN

Where women are concerned, no!

EMILY

Mother would have a fit.

THORSTEIN

[*Explodes.*] Oh, drop it, for God's sake, drop it! [Turns on ANDREW, *who is absorbed in his book again.*] Andrew, will you kindly take your long, blue nose out of that book for five seconds? Do you have to be the most promising instructor at Luther College twenty-four hours a day? What did you come here for?

ANDREW

I came, young man, to participate in a family rite known as the Graduation of the Family Genius.

THORSTEIN

I am not a genius. I am a mutant.

ANDREW

A what?

THORSTEIN

A mutant, a sport of nature, a two-headed calf.

ANDREW

Oh, you and your biology!

THORSTEIN

You and your Jesus Christ!

ANDREW

Well! I take it that this profanity found its inspiration in the Northfield lecture of Bjørnstierne Bjørnson.

THORSTEIN

In part.

ANDREW

You were not to go! Our synod forbade it.

THORSTEIN

So I heard.

ANDREW

He's an apostate and a heretic — and an out-and-out Darwinist!

THORSTEIN

So am I.

ANDREW

Great! Sensational! Call the press, sister Emily, to interview your brother, the famous heretic!

THORSTEIN

You don't have to. The press will hear all about it.

ANDREW

[*Realizing it is not a joke.*] What do you mean? The press will hear all about what?

THORSTEIN

About my views. They'll be presented at my public oration tomorrow.

ANDREW

With Mother and Father sitting there? You wouldn't!

THORSTEIN

Wait and see.

EMILY

Don't worry about it, Andrew. It's called "Mill's Examination of Hamilton's Philosophy of the Conditioned." No one will understand a word of it.

[*There is a knock at the door.* THORSTEIN *starts, then turns his back.* EMILY *goes to the door.* ANDREW *rises. Enter* ELLEN ROLFE. *She is not beautiful — but has a delicate, clever, and sensitive face. She is anything but a Norwegian type like* EMILY. ELLEN ROLFE *is wearing fine Sunday clothes, but her manner is free, friendly and natural.*]

EMILY

Welcome to the Clan Veblen!

ELLEN

Thank you, Emily. I'm sorry to be late.

EMILY

Late?

ELLEN

I told Thorstein about three.

THORSTEIN

No matter.

EMILY

Ellen, do you know our brother Andrew?

ELLEN

How do you do, Andrew? You were a figure on campus when I was just a freshman.

ANDREW

How do you do, Ellen? I believe we did meet once, as a matter of fact — at Professor Clark's house, I believe.

ELLEN

Oh, yes, of course.

ANDREW

There was no reason why you should have remembered.

EMILY

Tea, everybody? It's ready.

[*All but* THORSTEIN *say thanks and pull up chairs.* ELLEN *notices* THORSTEIN's *silence and bad manners.*]

ELLEN

Are you joining us, Thorstein?

THORSTEIN

Eventually.

ELLEN

I had trouble in getting here. My parents are here already for the grand commencement.

EMILY

Oh, you should have brought them along!

THORSTEIN

[*Sitting down to tea.*] Yes, you should have! . . . I could have slaughtered some neighborly pig and dug a barbecue pit in the middle of the room.

ELLEN

My parents were already committed to visit my uncle. I, too, it appeared, had been committed. How wise I was to run out on them!

THORSTEIN

I'm sorry, Ellen. I didn't really think you were coming.

ANDREW

Oh, but I was sure you would come. I told Thorstein . . .[*breaks off, embarrassed.*]

THORSTEIN

My brother understands young people.

ELLEN

[*To* ANDREW.] Aren't you on the faculty of Luther College now?

ANDREW

Why, yes, I am.

ELLEN

And do you like it?

ANDREW

Very much. But I find it taxing. I am giving six courses, in two of which, Latin composition and algebra, my preparation is decidedly slight.

THORSTEIN

Thank God for the other four courses.

ANDREW

[*To* ELLEN.] I hope you don't mind my brother's profanity.

ELLEN

Oh, I am quite used to it.

ANDREW

God is alway on his lips — but just before you arrived I had been given to understand that Thorstein, with the aid of Bjørnstierne Bjørnson and Charles Darwin, had abolished God.

ELLEN

Well, not quite. I believe Thorstein concedes His possibility.

ANDREW

[*To* THORSTEIN] Perhaps you prefer to call Him the Categorical Imperative?

THORSTEIN

[*Setting down his cup, rising.*] I do not. It is no improvement. People are ignorant and afraid. They conjure up Categorical Imperatives, angels, saints, tree-sprites, and other mystical creatures to protect them from the dark. All that explains nothing. It prevents explanations. When we find an explanation for anything —

why the dinosaurs died, why the waters receded from the continents, why the rabbits populated Australia, there are no angels or saints or tree-sprites in it.

ANDREW

No one is talking about tree-sprites. We're talking about God.

THORSTEIN

Same difference! God is a monopolist. He has put the tree-sprites out of business.

ELLEN

Now who is playing with language? Tree-sprites are mystical beings. God is a mystical being. Ergo, God is a big tree-sprite.

THORSTEIN

Well, what's wrong with that?

ELLEN

Let's try a different approach. Through all of time men have sensed the reality of God. Through time they have invented many names, many myths, to describe that unknown, and perhaps unknowable Reality. The names and myths are incidental. The Reality persists.

THORSTEIN

God persists as long as ignorance remains.

ELLEN

God persists as long as life has meaning, as long as life has value.

THORSTEIN

So meaning and value derive from God, and God derives from your sense of meaning and value!

ELLEN

Yes!

THORSTEIN

But every culture has its own meanings and values. So every culture invents its own gods.

ELLEN

But there is a God beyond all the separate gods. The God of life — and of love.

THORSTEIN

Poetic and beautiful. You have created God in your own image. But the world is not just love and beauty. It is a world where all living things kill all other living things. A world of hate and terror and murder.

ELLEN

It need not be!

THORSTEIN

It need be! It is part of life. You cannot make all of life into Sunday in a painted church below stained glass windows.

ELLEN

That too is a part of life.

THORSTEIN

I don't deny it. Life has millions of aspects, colors, shapes. Look then at *life*, at animals and at people, at cultures and institutions. Learn to live without God. Don't be afraid!

ANDREW

[*Rattling his teacup.*] I pity you! You are deaf, dumb and blind to what Ellen is saying.

THORSTEIN

[*Sitting down again.*] I shall try my best to learn from her in the future.

ELLEN

I'm afraid it's always the other way round.

EMILY

You should see them at parties — always off in a corner by themselves.

ELLEN

We are a campus scandal. The two Great Minds!

ANDREW

Ah, yes, there is nothing like the intellectual stimulation of good friends with different — eh — different points of view.

EMILY

[*Getting up to fetch teapot again.*] They're not so different as they sound!

ANDREW

Oh, they are. You and Thorstein could not be wider apart . . .

THORSTEIN

[*Balancing his cup in the air.*] Andrew, you should have been a ballet dancer. Such grace, such delicacy, such daring! I gasp at the way you capture the nuances of each situation.

ANDREW

What are you talking about?

THORSTEIN

[*Dropping his cup on the table.*] I am talking about a ballet dancer who has incredible skill at falling on his ass.

ANDREW

[*To Ellen.*] Please do not take offence at our loutish brother.

ELLEN

There is no one I am fonder of.

ANDREW

He's really not as terrible as he sounds.

ELLEN

I think he's worse!

ANDREW

Ellen, I am glad your parents were not here to be subjected to my brother's inimitable wit.

ELLEN

They might have enjoyed it . . . When are your own parents coming in?

EMILY

They should get here this evening.

ELLEN

I'm sure they must be really proud of our valedictorian.

THORSTEIN

Ah, yes. Country Bumpkin Makes Good. Of course, Andrew got there first.

ANDREW

Thorstein, why can't you ever let a thing alone? Why can't you let a thing be good and simple and nice?

THORSTEIN

Because, as I told you, I'm a freak. Because when everybody says yes, I say no. Because when everybody goes up, I go down. To hell with me! I am not interested in me. You would do me the greatest honor if you would never mention me, my name, my ideas, or my works again!

ANDREW

I will do my best. I will make every effort to consider you not as a brother but as a kind of infestation.

EMILY

Oh, Andrew, shut up!

ANDREW

Of course, our parents will not approve. They expect me to try to do something for you. But I will . . .

THORSTEIN

Oh, don't be so long-winded about it. Here, I'll save you time. Go to hell, Brother Andrew, go to hell! The feeling is mutual!

ANDREW

[*Ready to fight.*] Listen, Genius, if it weren't for Miss Rolfe's being here . . .

THORSTEIN

[*Getting to his feet.*] Oh, Miss Rolfe wouldn't mind, would you, Miss Rolfe?

EMILY

[*Coming between them.*] Oh, cut it out! Cut it out! [*Takes Andrew by his arm.*] A real Norwegian family reunion! Oh, day of joy! . . . Come on, Andy, we're taking a walk. Please!

ANDREW

All right. [*To* THORSTEIN.] I'll talk to you later. [*His embarrassment rises; he turns to* ELLEN.] Forgive me, Miss Rolfe . . . Ellen . . . This is not a usual sort of behavior for me . . .

THORSTEIN

Oh, go away!

ANDREW

Thorstein — see here. I'm sorry . . . Do you want to shake hands? [THORSTEIN *makes a face.*]

THORSTEIN

Oh, what the hell! [*Shakes hands with him.*] All right, forget it. Take a walk with your sister. You'll feel better.

ANDREW

[*Upset.*] Maybe we should. Excuse me, Ellen.

ELLEN

Surely.

EMILY

[*Cheerfully.*] See you later, Nellie!
[ANDREW *and* EMILY *leave.*]

ELLEN

What a business!

THORSTEIN

Sorry you had to be exposed to this.

ELLEN

What was it all about?

THORSTEIN

You.

ELLEN

But I thought you hadn't told your family anything . . .

THORSTEIN

I haven't. Andrew doesn't need instructions. He tends the household altar. He foresees the future. He has already begun to divest me of you.

ELLEN

But he only said . . .

THORSTEIN

Oh, the damned fool probably didn't know what he was doing himself . . . Oh, my God . . . [*He takes her in his arms; he is trembling.*]

ELLEN

What is it, my darling? What? What's wrong?

THORSTEIN

[*Releasing her.*] The whole thing. My parents, your parents. Me, you. The Norskies versus the Yankees. It gives me the shudders.

ELLEN

I know.

THORSTEIN

Will your family be as bad?

ELLEN

Worse. You're the inferior race, remember.

THORSTEIN

That doesn't make it worse. We are terribly proud of getting kicked. It makes us very exclusive.

ELLEN

It will be awful!

THORSTEIN

Ellen, I don't want to fight it out now. I have to give my oration. We have to graduate. This is not the time. Is it?

ELLEN

No. Not now. After all, why now? . . . Only if we wanted their help.

THORSTEIN

We don't want it, do we?

ELLEN

No. Please, no.

THORSTEIN

I couldn't ask your father. I can't ask mine. And we're not going to live on the farm, anyway. With you, or without you, I'm not going back to the farm.

ELLEN

Get a job and take me with you!

THORSTEIN

Doing what? With a stinking B.A. degree, who would want this Norskie? I've got to *get* somewhere first. I've got to *make* something of myself. I am not going into business. I'm a scholar, if anything. And I've got to be better than anybody else — and maybe that won't be good enough. But I've got to try. I've got to do graduate work. It's the only chance at a life for me or for us. Unless I can go on, there can't be a life for us, and I wouldn't be any good to you anyway.

ELLEN

I can wait. What else do I have to do?

THORSTEIN

It may be a long time, Ellen. It may be never. I don't want you to wait. I don't want to *feel* that waiting, weighing on me every moment of my life. Go on with your own life. Do whatever you want to do, wherever you want to do it. But don't wait for me.

ELLEN

All right. I will *not* wait. But come and take me when you are ready.

THORSTEIN

Ellen, I believe in myself. I know I can do it. I'll work hard.

ELLEN

I know.

THORSTEIN

I have a good head, don't I?

ELLEN

The best!

THORSTEIN

If that were only so . . . But it's not. Oh, if I could only tell you!

ELLEN

Tell me what?

THORSTEIN

What it's like to be me . . . I go around feeling wrong all the time. My face is wrong, my clothes are wrong, my speech is wrong. I'm never at home. Not with my family and not here. Sometimes I feel like a damned disembodied spirit. I feel . . . unclean. You can't know what that means. You were born right . . . I try to get out of it. I work hard, harder than I let on . . . but I don't feel as if I *know* anything. I'm always waiting for everybody to find me out.

ELLEN

You know more than anybody I ever met.

THORSTEIN

That's not what I mean . . . I mean: what I know is just a cover for what I don't know . . . All I really know is what's inside me — anger, self-pity, confusion.

ELLEN

Confusion about me?

THORSTEIN

Yes — about you, too . . . Ellen, what do you see in me?

ELLEN

I see a fine man.

THORSTEIN

I'm not a man. I'm a kid. I'm a big fake, that's what I am.

ELLEN

Most people feel that way.

THORSTEIN

Not the way I do. After a while they get it all covered up and stop feeling that way. They cover it up with a lot of habits and lies and furious activity. They cover it up with religion, with money, with liquor, with making babies, or maybe they just rot . . . I don't want to cover it up. I want to *know*. To find out what it's all about.

ELLEN

You will, I know you will!

THORSTEIN

But I want more. I want — you. Everything you stand for. I want to love you.

ELLEN

[Embracing him.] Yes, love me.

Scene 3

[The lights close in on them; then blackout. New light picks up the desk of the Rev. Noah Porter, President of Yale College. The time is now May, 1884. Porter, a corpulent man with mutton-chop whiskers, sits at his desk. Porter is fidgeting. He pulls his beard,

paces behind his desk, sits down again, takes a book out of a side-drawer, writes in the book. Then he pushes the button on his desk. Enter Porter's secretary; her manner is obsequious.]

SECRETARY

You rang, Dr. Porter?

PORTER

Please ask Mr. Veblen to come in.

SECRETARY

Yes, sir.
    [Exit secretary and enter Veblen, who is now almost twenty-seven. He is wearing drab, ill-fitting clothes. He is nervous.]

PORTER

Ah, Mr. Veblen, it was good of you to come so promptly. I had not meant my invitation to sound like a summons.

VEBLEN

It did not, sir. As a matter of fact, I have been most anxious to see you . . . I wanted . . . *[Interrupts himself. Sits awkwardly waiting for Porter to make the next move].*

PORTER

Yes, yes. Well, I sent for you, Mr. Veblen — I should be saying Dr. Veblen, shouldn't I? — to congratulate you personally on your doctoral examination. As you were informed by the secretary of the committee, your performance was considered to be excellent by all of us, although Professor Hitchcock was somewhat distressed at what he considered the *dogmatism* of your position.

VEBLEN

I am sorry if I gave that impression. My intention, on the contrary, was . . .

PORTER

. . . I know: to expose the fallacies of existing dogma. I myself thought that where Professor Hitchcock said "dogmatism" he might better have used "stubbornness," or even "boldness," and "intellectual courage".

VEBLEN

Thank you, sir.

PORTER

Professor Sumner, on the other hand, felt that your performance was *better* than excellent. He used the term "distinguished" and held that, together with Arthur Twining Hadley, you had written one of the two best dissertations ever done by a graduate student at Yale College. I think Sumner's right. As a matter of fact, I felt months ago that your performance would be memorable. You will recall that . . . *[glances at paper in front of him]* . . . on January 14, 1884, you asked me to write certain letters in support of your applications for teaching positions at several institutions. I thought that today might be a fitting occasion for you to hear just what I did write on your behalf.

VEBLEN

I should be most interested to hear.

PORTER

Good! *[reads]* "Mr. Thorstein Veblen has prosecuted special studies in Political and Social Science and in Speculative Philos-

ophy, ethics, psychology, etc. I can give confident testimony as to
his faithfulness and the critical ability which he has evinced in
all his studies. I have in all my experience had few pupils with
whom I have had greater satisfaction or who have made more
rapid or satisfactory progress . . ."

PORTER

You have more than amply justified it, Mr. Veblen . . . Well, and
what now?

VEBLEN

I don't know, sir.

PORTER

Don't know?

VEBLEN

I mean that I have not received an offer of a position.

PORTER

So I had feared, Mr. Veblen, so I had feared.

VEBLEN

You expected this?

PORTER

No, that is too strong. But, frankly, I had been somewhat appre-
hensive that there would be difficulty in placing you.

VEBLEN

But why, President Porter? You have said yourself . . .

PORTER

I know what I have said and what I have not said. I have said that Mr. Thorstein Bunde Veblen is very clever. I have not said that he is pushing in directions that pass beyond the limits of Christian belief — and in directions that I fear are strongly hostile to the American way of life. Mr. Veblen, I may tell you that, if I did not respect you as a man and a scholar, if I did not believe that ultimately you will get straightened out, I could make it impossible for you ever to receive an appointment in any respectable American institution.

VEBLEN

You are free to do your worst.

PORTER

Of course I am, young man. But I do not intend to.

VEBLEN

Because you want to save me?

PORTER

Put it that way if you like. [*Turns sideways to Veblen; takes book out of desk*]. See here, Veblen, I want you to have this — as a token of my respect and basic belief in you. It's Paul Janet's "On Morality". A wise little book! Read it!

VEBLEN

Thank you, sir . . . President Porter, please excuse my bluntness — but this means a great deal to me. To my family — and so on . . .

PORTER

I quite understand, my boy.

VEBLEN

Very well, then; you did not prevent my getting a job. But I got no job. Not a single offer of a job!

PORTER

Most unfortunate . . . Well, I too must be blunt. I presume your name — your national origin, and your failure to possess a divinity degree were all against you. Particularly in the field of philosophy.

VEBLEN

I had hoped Professor Sumner would find a place for me here.

PORTER

We considered that, Veblen. Considered it seriously. But Sumner has Hadley — and, well, I must be honest: you are not the Yale type, Veblen.

VEBLEN

[Losing hold of himself.] This is the crowning glory! It is not enough to say that I am un-Christian and un-American. But I am un-Yale!

PORTER

Veblen, like it or not, I have my responsibilities. I *am* charged with preserving the Christian character and the — gentlemanly atmosphere of this college . . . All right, let me say it for you: I am being terribly undemocratic, illiberal. But remember, Veblen, *I* am not Yale College. I am dependent upon the support of the trustees and our many donors. You must understand that *personally* I feel an occasional exception . . .

VEBLEN

Never mind, President Porter . . . I understand you perfectly. I understand that I have committed a terrible offense by subjecting religious belief to scientific analysis. I understand that I have sinned greatly in daring to criticize the dominance of money-men over the industrial development of this country. I can appreciate the unwillingness of those same money-men to give me employment in one of their seminaries of higher learning. I can understand that I am uncouth and have chosen the wrong parents. I can see that I am no gentleman. But I wish you had informed me of my unfitness for academic work three years ago!

PORTER

That is quite enough, Mr. Veblen, quite enough!

(CURTAIN)

ACT II

September, 1884

The Veblen farm in Wheeling township. Kari Veblen, now in her middle-fifties, is scouring pots. Thorstein, his face grayer and thinner than in the last scene, sits with a blanket wrapped around his legs and another over his shoulders, reading. It is early evening. Kari drops a pot. Thorstein looks up.

THORSTEIN
Mother, why don't you sit down for five minutes?

KARI
[Annoyed.] I have work to do. [Goes on working.]

THORSTEIN
[Looks down at his book again; then, after a few moments, looks up again.] Where is Father?

KARI
Playing games in the loft . . . Why don't you go up and play with him?

THORSTEIN
Mother, I'm sorry . . . How many times must I . . .

KARI
I know, I know . . . You're sick, you can't move, your legs ache you, your back aches you, your eyes are falling out . . .

THORSTEIN
Very funny. Malaria is the funniest thing in the world.

KARI

Malaria is not funny. But you don't have it.

THORSTEIN

Malaria sweeps the East coast, thousands die of it, I am there in the middle of the epidemic, but I — being a rock-ribbed Norwegian — could not possibly contract the slightest touch of malaria!

KARI

The doctor says you don't have it.

THORSTEIN

A country witch-doctor, what does he know? Why do you think I came home?

KARI

Do you want me to answer that?

THORSTEIN

Certainly, answer it!

KARI

Thorstein, you are my son and I am only going to say this to you: It's a lucky thing for you that you came out of a race and a family who have made a religion of family loyalty. I am disgusted, your father is disgusted, and your whole family is disgusted with this loafing of yours. You are the only loafer in a respectable community and a respectable family. It is shameful, shameful — especially now with your father working himself to death and worried sick over the panic . . .

[Noise at the door. Enter Thomas, looking much older. He goes to the sink to wash his hands. Dead silence greets him.]

THOMAS

All right, what's it all about?

KARI

What's what about?

THOMAS

I distinctly smelt something burning when I came in.

KARI

I shall look in the oven.

THORSTEIN

Mother is convinced I am a faker, a malingerer, a family parasite . . .

THOMAS

Kari, I have told you . . .

KARI

The doctor says there is nothing wrong with him.

THOMAS

The doctor is wrong. Such things have been known to happen. Thorstein is not well. Leave him alone, Kari!
[Dries his face, sits down tiredly near Thorstein.]

THORSTEIN

[With newspaper.] Price of wheat's still falling, I see . . . Down to 35 . . .

THOMAS

Only thing going up is freight rates . . . Can't hold my own. I'm working for nothing, less than nothing.

THORSTEIN

You'll never be a success, Father. You're not dishonest enough.

THOMAS

Same to you, son!

THORSTEIN

High praise indeed from a parent.

THOMAS

I mean it to be.

THORSTEIN

Two of a kind.

THOMAS

[Almost to himself.] One thing I wanted most in life: to be independent.

THORSTEIN

[Takes blanket from his feet, goes to sink to get himself a glass of water.] Father, that's the funniest thing you've said in a long time . . .

THOMAS

I guess I don't see the joke.

THORSTEIN

[With heavy irony.] Honorable Parent, it is fitting and proper that you should live in the illusion that you are that most blessed of men— the happy farmer; excuse me, the independent farmer. Thus will you sleepwalk to that destiny to which an all-seeing Providence has called you —and all the other independent farmers. Each will stand alone — at the mercy of any organization capable of mass action and a steady purpose. Thus will the pecuniary interests buy and sell and dispose of you and your goods on their own terms and at their own ease . . .

THOMAS

You think the game is rigged against us?

THORSTEIN

I know it is. The banks, the milling companies, the grain elevators, the railroads: all one big happy family. You carry them all on your back. And what do you get out of it?

THOMAS

A back-ache. You think I ought to get out? Go back to subsistence farming?

THORSTEIN

You can't get out. They won't let you. James J. Hill, Commodore Vanderbilt, Andrew Carnegie, John D. Rockefeller, and J. P. Morgan will not let you out. The whole deal depends on your participation in the game. Division of labor, Father! Principles of Economics, Lesson One! If you play the game their way, of your own free will, in your dream of being the independent farmer, you make it easy for them. But if you want out, then they will play rough. But the game will go on!

THOMAS

It can't go on forever. A man doesn't have the strength . . .

THORSTEIN

It won't go on forever. It's just a moment in time.

THOMAS

No wonder they loved you at Yale! . . . Well, son, what are *you* going to do about it?

THORSTEIN

I don't know. How can I stop it? The process is running fast. It can smash up, it can become something else. We can go back to a rule of force, status, and the dark ages. Or we can see the full development of an industrial republic, where the workers, the farmers, the engineers, the *creators* will govern themselves. Both these tendencies are powerful. Which of the two is stronger in the long run is a blind guess — but the future — so far as I can see — belongs to one or the other.

THOMAS

You want to go on studying all that?

THORSTEIN

If possible.

KARI

[*Who has been listening at her work.*] If you have any decency, you'll forget about the studying for a while and help your father now when he needs you.

THOMAS

I don't need Thorstein. Besides, what he has to do is much more important.

THORSTEIN

It's an academic question, Mother. No university will give me a job . . . You're right — I am useless, completely useless — to my family and to myself ... *[Pause]* ... also to a certain female who is expecting me to marry her.

[Pause; mood changes]

KARI

So the letter *was* from a girl?

THORSTEIN

It was.

KARI

Who is she?

THORSTEIN

Her name is Ellen Rolfe. I knew her at Carleton.

KARI

Rolfe? A Norwegian girl?

THORSTEIN

The girl is in a sense a product of Norway. Her name, I have discovered, goes back to the first Viking chief, Gange Rolfe, who pillaged Normandy. The descendants of Gange Rolfe conquered England and their descendants became the ruling stock of New England.

KARI

So she's a Yankee!

THORSTEIN

Yes, Mother, she's a damned Yankee.

KARI

Your own kind are not good enough for you.

THORSTEIN

I am not good enough for my own kind.

KARI

What does her father do?

THORSTEIN

He's a railroad man.

KARI

An engineer, a conductor? What kind of railroad man?

THORSTEIN

A vice-president of the Santa Fe. Her uncle is the president of the Santa Fe. Another of her uncles is the president of Carleton College.

KARI

And she wants to marry you? Is she all there in the head?

THORSTEIN

Probably not.

THOMAS

And you, Thorstein? Do you want to marry the Santa Fe Railroad? After what you said?

THORSTEIN

I do not want to marry the Santa Fe Railroad. I want to marry Ellen Rolfe, daughter of Gange Rolfe.

THOMAS

What do you intend to do to support her?

THORSTEIN

A good question. I like that question.

THOMAS

I am serious.

THORSTEIN

The young lady has spoken to her father. That gentleman, recognizing as my mother does that his daughter is not all there and thus requires certain care and indulgence, is willing to consent to the marriage and to offer me employment as economist for the Santa Fe Railroad.

THOMAS

Surely you will not take the job?

THORSTEIN

Such a decision depends on the interplay of certain social and economic forces. If history wants it otherwise, let history decide!

THOMAS

But unless you find something else, you have decided to marry her and take the job?

THORSTEIN

If I can secure the blessings of my parents.

THOMAS

This is not like you, Thorstein. It is not honorable.

THORSTEIN

Is it more honorable to take a position, if I could get one, in some seminary of the higher learning, bought and paid for by the Santa Fe Railroad and its corporate cousins?

THOMAS

You exaggerate. In this country there is still freedom. Freedom to say what you want. Freedom to teach what you want. All right, so it is hard to get a job. But to teach at a college or university is not the same as to be a kept economist for the railroads.

THORSTEIN

I will go on trying to get a teaching job.

THOMAS

Good.

KARI

What is she like, this girl?

THORSTEIN

She's very smart.

KARI

Then she is not for you.

THOMAS

Kari!

KARI

Can she cook, can she clean a house, can she sew?

THOMAS

He wants a wife, not a housemaid.

KARI

I know your son better than you. He wants a housemaid, not a wife.

THORSTEIN

Excuse me — I feel sick.

KARI

You should!

[Thorstein leaves the room by the outside door.]

THOMAS

Kari, this is no way!

KARI

He is killing me.

THOMAS

He is not killing you. He is not doing anything to you. Can't you see that the boy has had a terrible time? Years he worked and then they hand him a two-dollar book and say, "Disappear. Go back to your farm."

KARI

It is a terrible thing they have done!

THOMAS

They will suffer for it.

KARI

No, *they* will not suffer. It is he who will suffer, and we who will suffer. He will go out of his mind.

THOMAS

If you see this, why don't you leave him in peace? Why must you hurt him so?

KARI

I don't want to hurt him. I can't control myself. I want to stop him from doing it. I want to wake him up, bring him to his senses!

THOMAS

It is no way!

KARI

He is ruining his life. He is so bitter. It is a terrible thing to hate.
I don't care what they have done. He must not hate!

THOMAS

He needs love.

KARI

He needs God, he needs God's love!

THOMAS

If there is a God, he has God's love.

KARI

He has denied Him! This is his punishment!

THOMAS

You are cursing him.

KARI

I am not, I am not! *[weeps]* . . . I want to save him!

THOMAS

It is too late for you. He is not a child any more. His mother and
father cannot save him. He must save himself. Let him go!

KARI

He will destroy himself.

THOMAS

We must run that risk.

KARI

I don't even know the girl. I don't want to say anything against her. But I feel in my heart that this is wrong, that she is not for him.

THOMAS

You are speaking from prejudice. It is only because she is a Yankee.

KARI

Those women don't know how to treat a man, they don't know what a man is. They think only of themselves.

THOMAS

She is not "those women". She is a girl who loves our son, a girl he loves.

KARI

He doesn't know what he loves — or *if* he loves. He has learned only to hate. That is what they have taught him in their fine universities!

THOMAS

Nonsense!

KARI

He is all mixed up. He is coming to hate himself. He wants to escape. He wants to go into their world and escape. Because they have done this to him, he wants to marry one of them — in spite. To live and work among them — in spite and hatred, sneering at them . . . He must come back to his own kind and find peace and love!

THOMAS

He cannot. It is too late.

KARI

It is not too late. It is your duty as a father to stop him.

THOMAS

It is my duty as a father to let him become a man.

KARI

Thomas, you are wrong, *wrong!* This is no time for your big ideas! This is our son, at a terrible time in his life! Our own son at a time when he cannot think for himself. This is a girl who is no good for him. This is hate, hate, not love! He never *said* he loved her, he never *showed* he loved her.

THOMAS

He didn't have a chance. We will ask him.

KARI

Yes, ask him! When you want to know something, just ask a question. Don't think, don't feel, just ask!

THOMAS

Yes, ask! Look to *him* . . . don't look just to yourself.

KARI

There is another I can look to, another I can ask . . . *[raises her hands in prayer, bows her head.]* Dear God, hear me. My son has sinned, sinned in his passion and in his blindness. It is not his fault, God. An awful wrong has been done him. Our enemies have hurt him. They have torn at him and hurt him. In his anger and hatred he does not know what he is doing. Help him. Have mercy upon him and his parents. Take him back. Save him for his people. Save him from the ruin he is seeking. Show him the light. Lift the scales from his eyes. *[While she is praying, Thorstein enters; he looks pale and sick; his expression becomes one of revulsion as he takes in the scene.]* Show him the path to repentance. This I ask in Jesus' name. Amen. *[Lowers her hands.]*

THORSTEIN

[Sarcastically.] The last refuge.

KARI

Yes — my last refuge!

THORSTEIN

It is too late. I am going to marry her.

BLACKOUT

Scene 2

The lights come up on the kitchen of the farm of Thorstein and Ellen Rolfe Veblen at Stacyville, Minnesota. Except for the books in packing-crates against the wall, the room looks like an ordinary farm kitchen. The time is August, 1891, seven years after the last scene. Kari and Thomas are seated in straight-backed chairs, wearing "visiting" clothes. Thorstein is standing. He is wearing a woolen lumber-jacket and corduroy trousers.

THORSTEIN

[Calls.] Ellen, Ellen! Will you please come here?
[Enter Ellen, a woman of thirty-two, rather pale and worn. She is wearing a simple black dress.]

ELLEN

I'm sorry, Thorstein . . .

THORSTEIN

Forget Emily's letter! Do you realize how long you've been gone? You know Mother and Father have to be starting back . . .

ELLEN

I'm sorry. I thought I knew where it was. I can't seem to lay my hands on it.

THOMAS

It is nothing, Ellen.

THORSTEIN

Can't you just tell them what she said?

ELLEN

Oh, it wasn't so much what she said. It was just about the children and about wanting to come to see us. But it was all so warm and happy . . .

KARI

My Emily is a good girl. She has three nice children.

ELLEN

Where is Andrew?

THORSTEIN

You took so long. He's out hitching up the horses.

ELLEN

I'm sorry. It's such an awful feeling — when you were sure you had something and then you search and search but you can't find it. It always upsets me.

THOMAS

I am the same.

KARI

We have kept everything, everything from the old country.

THOMAS

Thorstein . . .

THORSTEIN

Yes, Father?

THOMAS

Thorstein, you do not look well.

THORSTEIN

It's nothing. I've had a cold.

ELLEN

Is it too cold in the house?

KARI

No, we are used to it.

THOMAS

I wish I could say something . . .

ELLEN

What is it, Father?

THOMAS

Impossible!

[Enter Andrew Veblen, rubbing his arms.]

ANDREW

Phew . . . it's chilly out already. Looks like an early winter.

THOMAS

[Standing up.] We better start. It is a long drive.

KARI

Yes, we better go. *[She stands up, goes for her coat. Thorstein
helps her, and fetches his father's coat.]*

ANDREW

You sure you don't want me to drive back with you?

THOMAS

No, no. You spend the night here. You got things to do.

ANDREW

Did you say anything?

THOMAS

No.

ELLEN

Mother, don't forget your knitting.

KARI

I do not forget things.

　　　[They are getting into their coats.]

THORSTEIN

[Holding his father's coat for him.] If it's getting cold out,
maybe you'd do better to stay over and drive back in the morning.

THOMAS

No, we must go.

ELLEN

It was wonderful to have you with us.

KARI

Ellen, you are getting to be a good cook.

ELLEN

Thank you . . . I'm sorry it took so long.

THOMAS

Well, take care of yourselves. Come to us soon!

THORSTEIN

Soon as we can make it. Come, I'll help you into the carriage.

KARI

No, if you got a cold, stay in.

THORSTEIN

Oh, for two seconds, what is it?

ANDREW

I can do it.

THORSTEIN

All right. Goodbye!
[Kari, Thomas and Andrew go out; Ellen goes to the sink and begins to wash the dishes.]

ELLEN

Oh, I could die!

THORSTEIN

Oh, let her alone. She's an old woman.

ELLEN

I let *her* alone!

THORSTEIN

[Goes to the window.] They're going! *[Waves.]* Ellen! *[She joins him at the window, waving.]*

ELLEN

[Leaving the window.] Always the same, always the same.
[Enter Andrew from outdoors; his face is grave.]

THORSTEIN

Thanks, Andy. I did feel a bit chilled . . . Well, what was the parting shot?

ANDREW

Thorstein, Father is worried about you.

THORSTEIN

I'm all right.

ANDREW

Not your cold. He wanted to say something to you. I guess he didn't like to . . . in front of Ellen. Excuse me, Ellen . . . I only mean . . .

ELLEN

[Turning away from the dishes.] Never mind. What is he disturbed about?

ANDREW

Thorstein. His frame of mind, his inactivity. Father thinks it is time it ceased.

THORSTEIN

Time it ceased! What does he suggest I do — take dancing lessons?

ANDREW

He thinks you belong at a university.

THORSTEIN

A brilliant idea! Well, which chair shall I take — the professorship of philosophy at Harvard or the professorship of political economy at Yale?

ANDREW

Don't make a joke of everything.

THORSTEIN

So this is what it was all about! *[Laughs.]* Andrew, Andrew, what do you think you are telling me?

ANDREW

For once in your life . . .

THORSTEIN

All right, what do you want me to do about it? You know I've tried everything. Carleton wouldn't take me, Yale wouldn't touch me with a ten-foot pole. Who would? I even tried to crawl back into the fold — to St. Olaf. They smelled my agnosticism — no deal! I wrote letters, I had letters written, I travelled to Iowa, to Texas. What came of it all?

ANDREW

Nothing.

THORSTEIN

Maybe you have a job for me?

ANDREW

No.

THORSTEIN

Then what? What are you getting at?

ANDREW

You must go back as a student.

THORSTEIN

As a student! Ellen, you hear this?

ELLEN

Andrew, this is preposterous. [*Goes to Thorstein.*] How can you say such a thing to him? He has more brains in his little finger than the professors have in their fat heads! You should have better sense. Thorstein should not be humiliated!

ANDREW

I am not trying to humiliate him. I am only trying . . .

ELLEN

You come to him, secure and comfortable, and your very presence is enough . . . No, Andrew, use your head . . .

ANDREW

You have become as wild as he is!

THORSTEIN

[Starts deliberately, builds up.] Andrew, you've got it backwards. You're the one who's being wild. Just look at the situation exactly as it is. Seven years ago I got my Ph.D. Seven stinking years ago. Very well, I didn't get a job but neither did I lose my mind. I have been reading, writing, growing — *growing*, I say . . . I know what has been happening to me! Ellen, is it true?

ELLEN

Yes, it's true!

THORSTEIN

For seven years I thought to myself: Well, at least you are growing, you are going deeper than you ever could have gone in any other way. It's rotten but it's the cost you have to pay. They kicked you out but one day you will come back and they will see. They will find out who you are! I have waited for the day and waited. I have thought, I have worked, I know what I know! . . . And so at last comes the learned brother with his brilliant plan: I shall again become the pupil of the distinguished charlatans of American education. I will sit at their scented feet, catch crumbs from their table. You think they have starved me out, I am ready to capitulate, they can take me! Well, you are wrong, Andrew, wrong as hell! I am not broken!

ANDREW

Thorstein, you are raving.

THORSTEIN

I would rather die on this farm.

ANDREW

You misunderstand me completely. I am only trying to be practical. This useless, empty life of yours must come to an end. Nothing has come of it.

THORSTEIN

How do you know what has come of it?

ANDREW

Well, what have you done? Show me something!

THORSTEIN

That is stupid! Here, look in my ear and see for yourself!

ANDREW

Inside is worthless, Thorstein. It must come out. You must go back. It is the only way you can go back — as a student.

THORSTEIN

[*Turns his back.*] I am through listening to you. I have nothing more to say.

ELLEN

And what if he did go back as a student? Then what, Andrew?

ANDREW

Then they *would* see his value. All right, I believe him! He *has* grown. This time they will not be able to deny him.

ELLEN

Why not? Then, he was seven years younger. Then, he was not finally committed. They could have deceived themselves, if they

had wanted to. Then, he had just written his thesis; they said it
was brilliant. He had just published the paper on Kant in their
best journal; they said it was a real contribution! That was seven
years ago — and nothing came of it. What can he expect from
them now?

ANDREW

Ellen, I had hoped for your support.

ELLEN

Thorstein has my support.

ANDREW

Thorstein, will you listen to me? [THORSTEIN *says nothing.*] All
right, don't listen to me. But listen to your father! He has never
said this kind of thing to you before. He made only one decision
for you — to send you to Carleton. Since then he has never inter-
fered. He left you free to make your own decisions — to go to
Yale, to marry Ellen, to live here, to do nothing, to do whatever
you wanted. Now he has told me to say he wants you to go back.
He *asks* you to go back. He says he has some savings and he wants
you to take them and go back to a university. He says it will mean
very much to him.

[*This hits* THORSTEIN *deeply; he rubs his eyes wearily —
speaks deliberately, hollowly.*]

THORSTEIN

He should never have sent me to college in the first place. You
tell him . . .

ANDREW

[*Furious, now bursts out.*] You tell him yourself! You face him, you show him what a fool he's been!

THORSTEIN

Idiocy, plain idiocy.

ANDREW

[*Trying to regain control.*] I am very nervous, Thorstein . . . Don't misunderstand me . . . Thorstein . . . Just promise me one thing: that you will . . . think about it.

THORSTEIN

I will promise you nothing.

ANDREW

I didn't think . . . I don't mean . . .

THORSTEIN

Oh, go take a walk! Leave me alone!

ANDREW

As you say . . .
 [*Exit.*]

THORSTEIN

Ellen, for God's sake, look at this place! It's a pig-sty! Dishes all over the sink! . . . Ellen, are you listening to me?

ELLEN

I hear every word you say . . . Why do you have to let it out on me?

THORSTEIN

Let it out on you? Are you involved in my life or not?

ELLEN

So it seems.

THORSTEIN

What do you all want from me?

ELLEN

Nothing, Thorstein, nothing. Only that you find your place.

THORSTEIN

I don't want a life based on lies and illusions. Look at what they did to your father. He was a great man — until they took away his railroad!

ELLEN

My father was a man of honor. When he saw it happening, he could have watered the stock and come out a rich man.

THORSTEIN

He was a tiger without teeth. He should never have believed his own nonsense about the ethics of business. He was a fool.

ELLEN

How can you be so cruel?

THORSTEIN

I am not being cruel. I am simply making an objective statement of fact. You are a worse fool than he was. The cruellest thing in this world, it turns out, is to maintain one's objectivity and look directly at the facts.

ELLEN

You are good at that.

THORSTEIN

I owe it all to the crooks who took the railroad away from your father. I shall never stop being grateful to them for preventing me, in my hour of imbecility, from taking a job as whore-economist on the Santa Fe.

ELLEN

The hour of imbecility in which you married me.

THORSTEIN

That was simply a contemporaneous event.

ELLEN

You've hated the years on this farm.

THORSTEIN

The years on this farm, yes. Had you expected me to love these years of idleness and waste?

ELLEN

They needn't have been.

THORSTEIN

Waste. Nothing but waste. To hell with it. It's over.

Scene 3

Fade and blackout. Lights go up on another college office, that of Professor J. Laurence Laughlin. It is now a few weeks later — mid-September, 1891; the place is Cornell University, Ithaca, New

York. Laughlin, well-dressed, well-barbered, looks more like a businessman than a professor. He is concentrating hard on something he is reading at his desk. Enter VEBLEN — *wearing a coonskin cap and corduroy trousers.*

VEBLEN

[*In a mild, slightly ironic tone.*] I am Thorstein Veblen.

LAUGHLIN

[*Startled.*] What?

VEBLEN

[*A bit louder.*] I am Thorstein Veblen.

LAUGHLIN

Well, that's just fine. Now please tell me who in blazes is Thorstein Veblen?

VEBLEN

I am a farmer. I live on a farm in Stacyville, Minnesota. My parents have a farm in Wheeling township, Minnesota. They are Norwegian immigrants to this country.

LAUGHLIN

I see, I see . . . Sit down, my good fellow!

VEBLEN

If you don't mind, I'd just as soon stand.

LAUGHLIN

As you like.

VEBLEN

Do you want to hear anything else?

LAUGHLIN

Anything you feel like telling me.

VEBLEN

I got a B.A. at Carleton College in 1880 and a Ph.D. at Yale in 1884. My degree was in philosophy but I'm interested in economics, sociology, anthropology, biology and languages. I know German, French, Spanish, Italian, Dutch, and the Scandinavian languages, including Icelandic . . . Are you sure that you want to hear all this?

LAUGHLIN

I do. On one condition: that you take off that damned coonskin hat and have a cigar.

VEBLEN

All right. [*Sits down, accepts cigar, gets light.*]

LAUGHLIN

What was your doctoral dissertation on?

VEBLEN

The title was "Ethical Grounds of a Doctrine of Redemption." It was considered agnostic. It was. And I am.

LAUGHLIN

You write it under Noah Porter?

VEBLEN

Yes.

LAUGHLIN

He couldn't have liked it.

VEBLEN

He didn't. I didn't get a job.

LAUGHLIN

So then what did you do?

VEBLEN

Nothing.

LAUGHLIN

What do you mean?

VEBLEN

I mean I never got a job.

LAUGHLIN

Where did you try?

VEBLEN

Everywhere.

LAUGHLIN

You ever been in any trouble?

VEBLEN

No. Not counting a few fist-fights.

LAUGHLIN

Veblen! Are you the Veblen who did that article on Kant . . .
one of the fancy journals . . . 1883 or '84?

VEBLEN

'84. Journal of Speculative Philosophy.

LAUGHLIN

What have you done since?

VEBLEN

Nothing. I told you.

LAUGHLIN

Oh, cut it out, man!

VEBLEN

I got sick; I got married. My wife's father gave us a farm. I've been on the farm.

LAUGHLIN

Reading?

VEBLEN

Mostly.

LAUGHLIN

You kept trying for an academic job?

VEBLEN

For the first six years.

LAUGHLIN

Hmm. You can't think much of American education.

VEBLEN

I don't. But I try to be objective. I see it as part of a larger whole.

LAUGHLIN

Oho! That makes it worse! . . . And what do you think is wrong with the whole and its various parts?

VEBLEN

Domination by businessmen and bankers . . . This was supposed to be the country without classes, the country where all men were held to be created free and equal. Now the country has a leisure class sitting on top of it. A leisure class whose power comes from their control of financial institutions, not from their fighting prowess, possession of land, or divine ordination like earlier leisure classes. But the grip of ours is just as strong and they're squeezing the life out of this country.

LAUGHLIN

Bang, bang, bang, just like that . . . I like your guts. Do you know who I am?

VEBLEN

The professor of political economy.

LAUGHLIN

Do you also know that I have been president of the Philadelphia Mutual Insurance Company? Do you know that I am still a member of its board? Do you know that I am one of your arch-monsters?

VEBLEN

Nothing monstrous. It's just a cultural phase.

LAUGHLIN

A cultural phase! I wouldn't know about that. I only know economics. I have no sympathy with this notion of mixing economics up with all this other stuff — philosophy, history, sociology, biology, anatomy, and what have you. My economic thinking stops roughly with John Stuart Mill — only I have tried to clean Mill up. I have written an abridgement of Mill's *Principles*, cutting out all the metaphysical nonsense, and I use it as my text.

VEBLEN

That's funny.

LAUGHLIN

It gets funnier. I believe in God and our Lord Jesus Christ.

VEBLEN

[*Starting to get up.*] Well, I guess . . .

LAUGHLIN

Wait! I'm not finished. You haven't heard anything about *my* family. I'm the son of immigrants, too, only mine came from Ireland. My father got to be the mayor of Alliance, Ohio. My family believes and I believe in American democracy. I think you are all wet, Dr. Thorstein Veblen, and I want a chance to prove it to you. I think we can make it a fair fight. Nothing I like more! Now then, just what is it you want from me, Dr. Veblen?

VEBLEN

A fellowship. I want to come back to the university and I don't want to use my father's small savings.

LAUGHLIN

Then, later, I suppose you intend to weasel your way into an academic post?

VEBLEN

That's what I had in mind.

LAUGHLIN

Good idea. But it's September, man, and all our fellowships have been filled.

VEBLEN

I see . . . [*Stands up.*]

LAUGHLIN

However, I will see what can be done. [*Stands up.*] I want you to stay right here while I go down to the President's office and, if necessary, to all the other high and mighty powers of Cornell University and make them give me a special grant for you.

VEBLEN

They'll never do it.

LAUGHLIN

They'll do it — or I'm going back to the insurance business and take my ill-gotten gains with me. This *is* a free country, Veblen, and this is a free university, and I mean to keep you away from that farm in Minnesota before you blow us all up . . . [*Three steps towards the door, then turns again.*] And when the time comes, we'll see what we can weasel you into . . . As it happens, I'm an old weasel myself! [*Exit.*]

[VEBLEN *stands there, looking at his coonskin hat; deliberately puts the hat on his head, and sits down.*]

BLACKOUT

Scene 4

The farm in Stacyville, three weeks later. THORSTEIN *and* ELLEN
*are finishing the job of packing up, for the move to Ithaca. The
floor is littered with boxes, paper, books, and household goods.*

THORSTEIN

Do we really need all this stuff?

ELLEN

What else can we do with it — throw it away?

THORSTEIN

Can't we sell some of it?

ELLEN

To whom?

THORSTEIN

I can talk to Joe Hansen. As long as they're renting the place . . .

ELLEN

Well, it's worth a try.

THORSTEIN

There just won't be room for so much junk in the place in Ithaca.

ELLEN

That box is for the loft. The rest is just what we absolutely need
— clothing, books, kitchen things . . .

THORSTEIN

You don't seem to realize how small the place is.

ELLEN

Oh, we'll manage, I'm sure.

THORSTEIN

It's really just one room and a kitchen. Practically no closet space.

ELLEN

I just wish you had a better place to work. Can't they give you an office?

THORSTEIN

I have one! Wait till you see it! It's about half the size of this room and I have to share it with only three other graduate assistants. School-boys . . . But what the hell . . . I can work at the library.

ELLEN

I'm sure we can fix up a desk for you in the apartment.

THORSTEIN

We'll see . . .

ELLEN

Are you worried?

THORSTEIN

About that? No . . . It will be all right.

ELLEN

Laughlin sounds like such a fine man.

THORSTEIN

He is . . . He thinks I'm crazy but it doesn't seem to worry him. He's an old-fashioned liberal, you know — a pre-industrial revolution liberal — an "I disagree with everything you have to say but I will defend to the death your right to say it" kind of liberal.

ELLEN

What more would you want?

THORSTEIN

Nothing more — of him! But wait till you see the rest of the department! The usual assortment of mush-mouths and mush-rooms. They look at me like something with eight legs.

ELLEN

They'll find out who you are.

THORSTEIN

Maybe . . . Ellen, I've got so much to do. I feel as if I'm starting from nowhere. I'm afraid I'm going to be hard to live with for a while. I'm so keyed up already. Ellen, honestly, I'm worried. I've just been realizing what this means. I never thought I'd have a chance. But for some damned reason, Laughlin is sold on me . . . Well, let's start cleaning up this mess.

ELLEN

[*Sitting down.*] Just a moment, Thorstein.

THORSTEIN

What's the matter — exhausted?

ELLEN

Yes, I . . . I am not feeling well.

THORSTEIN

Are you getting sick?

ELLEN

No. Not sick.

THORSTEIN

What is it, for God's sake?

ELLEN

[*Blurting it out.*] I'm pregnant.

THORSTEIN

[*Reacting dully.*] What?

ELLEN

Pregnant.

THORSTEIN

How do you know?

ELLEN

[*Fearfully, angrily.*] How do you think I know?

THORSTEIN

How long has it been?

ELLEN

Almost two months.

THORSTEIN

That doesn't necessarily mean anything.

ELLEN

Is that all you have to say to me?

THORSTEIN

What do you expect me to say?

ELLEN

I thought you'd be . . . glad . . .

THORSTEIN

What's there to be glad about? . . . Oh, God, I might have known it couldn't last! This is my fantastic luck! Just when I thought it was changing . . . I should have known . . .

ELLEN

[*Furious.*] I knew it! I knew you'd be like this. I didn't know how to tell you. I was afraid to. I didn't want to write . . . I prayed . . .

THORSTEIN

Prayed! A lot of good that does!

ELLEN

I didn't know what else to do.

THORSTEIN

Pregnant! Now, of all times!

ELLEN

I'm sorry.

THORSTEIN

Where are we supposed to put a baby in that hole? How am I supposed to work? What are we supposed to use for money?

ELLEN

I can work.

THORSTEIN

How am I supposed to think? How am I supposed to concentrate?

ELLEN

Please, Thorstein, please! Don't get excited!

THORSTEIN

Excited! You greet me with this announcement out of the blue and I'm supposed to lie down and have my first good night's sleep!

ELLEN

And what am *I* supposed to do? What do you want me to do?

THORSTEIN

Don't ask me. Ask a doctor.

ELLEN

I want the baby! I want him!

THORSTEIN

Oh, God, God, God! Listen to this!

ELLEN

What is the sense of raving? What good will that do?

THORSTEIN

No Goddamned good at all!

ELLEN

I'll thank you not to swear just now.

THORSTEIN

Aren't we getting holy now that motherhood approaches!

ELLEN

I've never stopped believing. Never.

THORSTEIN

As if I didn't know.

ELLEN

I'm terribly sorry. I hope you will forgive me for believing in God.

THORSTEIN

You're forgiven.

ELLEN

Now should I ask God to forgive me for believing in Veblen.

THORSTEIN

That's harder to forgive. But I'm sure He pities you. What did you marry me for in the first place? That's a question that interests me.

ELLEN

I know only one answer. I'm sure you'd find it unbearably sentimental.

THORSTEIN

I would. Because I'm interested in the real reason.

ELLEN

What do you want me to say?

THORSTEIN .

Why you wanted me. Why you were willing to lower yourself. Were your own men too stupid? Were they too clean? Were you sick of being pure? Are you satisfied now — are you adequately defiled?

ELLEN

Why do you hurt me so? Why do you hate me?

THORSTEIN

Hate — love. I'm not capable of either one.

ELLEN

Is that my fault, too?

THORSTEIN

My fault, your fault. That everlasting Christian sense of guilt! *That's* why you married me, if you want to know! You pitied me. You saw what your countrymen were doing to me. It made you suffer. You expiated the sin by marrying me.

ELLEN

And why did you marry *me?* To help me expiate the sin?

THORSTEIN

Yes, as an act of revenge.

ELLEN

That's a lie!

THORSTEIN

My mother said so from the beginning. I wouldn't face it then, but she was right.

ELLEN

It's a lie, you know it's a lie!

THORSTEIN

I thought you were the least hysterical female I had met.

ELLEN

You thought I wouldn't interfere with your work.

THORSTEIN

That's what I thought.

ELLEN

What do you think a marriage is for?

THORSTEIN

A marriage? It's a way of avoiding the police.

ELLEN

It's not to have children?

THORSTEIN

Go marry the dogs and cats.

ELLEN

You're sterile, you're dry, you're dead!

THORSTEIN

That's right. And God help any child I father.

ELLEN

This isn't you. This isn't the man I married.

THORSTEIN

Unfortunately it is. I tried to tell you a long time ago. You wouldn't listen to me. I told you to get out. No, you had to have it your way. Now you know. Now you see what I am.

ELLEN

It's not you.

THORSTEIN

You'll get used to the idea. It took seven years to get this far.

ELLEN

[*Moving to him, her hand on his arm.*] I'll never believe it. I know who you are.

THORSTEIN

[*Thrusting her hand away.*] It's no use, Ellen. This time you can't do it.

ELLEN

[*Starting to cry.*] Oh, my God, what am I going to do?

THORSTEIN

Do? Have your baby. Then you won't need me. He'll give you what I can't.

ELLEN

You're crazy, crazy . . .

THORSTEIN

The best I can wish him is that he never knows his father.

ELLEN

Without you I don't want him.

THORSTEIN

Tricks, lies!

ELLEN

For what you're doing to me you'll suffer.

THORSTEIN

Up and down, up and down, listen to you! I can't stand this. I'm getting out of here.

ELLEN

[*Cries helplessly.*]

THORSTEIN

That's right. Turn it on! Full blast! All you've got! Every woman knows how. Tear me open! Show me what I am!

ELLEN

I'm sick, I'm sick!

THORSTEIN

[*Clapping his hands over his ears.*] Shut up, for God's sake, shut up!

ELLEN

Don't scream at me! Please, Thorstein, please . . .

[*She staggers, grabs for a chair, lowers herself to her knees sobbing.*]

CURTAIN

ACT III

April, 1906.

The living-room-study of the apartment of THORSTEIN *and* ELLEN VEBLEN *in Chicago. Four men are sitting rather stiffly in a semi-circle. They are Professors* LAUGHLIN, LASSITER, THAYER *and* BALDWIN. *The men are talking somewhat warily, their eyes turning to the door leading to the back of the apartment.* LASSITER *is about fifty years old,* THAYER *about forty, and* BALDWIN *about thirty.*

LASSITER

Genius or no genius, he certainly has poor manners!

LAUGHLIN

We probably shouldn't have barged in on him.

THAYER

We came as his friends. He has a right to know what is going on.

LAUGHLIN

I am sure he knows.

LASSITER

Well, he wasn't at the faculty meeting, so he doesn't know the latest.

BALDWIN

Probably doesn't give a damn.

LASSITER

Oh, he gives a damn. If he gets the sack, he'll give a damn.

THAYER

What time is it?

BALDWIN

Almost five.

THAYER

How long is he going to leave us sitting here like fools? We've got the Dean coming to dinner tonight . . . I really can't stay much longer.

LAUGHLIN

I'm sure he won't mind if you run along.

THAYER

It's these little things that make him so impossible.

LASSITER

They're not so little. He refuses to be part of a community. Other people serve on committees of the faculty; Assistant Professor Veblen is much too important to serve on a committee. Other people attend football games and support the team; Assistant Professor Veblen regards sport as barbaric.

THAYER

Other professors entertain their colleagues, members of the Administration, and influential persons from the community. And Veblen . . .

BALDWIN

. . . And Veblen says to hell with them. And I say good for him! He's the only one with any guts.

LASSITER

Poppycock! What has guts got to do with it? All of these activities are part of the university's life. We have a mission to perform. We must give what we have learned to the general community.

BALDWIN

Ah . . .

LASSITER

You whippersnappers can laugh at us who spend our spare time speaking before ladies' clubs and Rotary meetings, but if this university has a good name it is thanks to us, not to the bookworms who spend their lives scribbling articles for journals that nobody reads. Who pays your salary? The Quarterly Journal of Economics? Not on your hat!

LAUGHLIN

Well, really, Lassiter, you are . . .

LASSITER

I know, I am going too far. Certainly, research is important. But everything in proportion. And Veblen refuses to do anything, *anything!*

BALDWIN

Anything but turn economic theory upside down and inside out. Anything but expose the rotten foundations of our so-called science: the nonsense that the mind of man is an adding machine. Veblen has destroyed economic man. He has restored man as he *is* to the social sciences!

LASSITER

Ah, the voice of the disciple!

BALDWIN

I am not ashamed of it.

LAUGHLIN

I don't know that man-as-he-is matters so much to economic theory. We are interested simply in man's economic behavior — how he responds to price changes, how he chooses among economic goods, how he reacts to opportunities for profits, wage increases, et cetera. Veblen wants to make economics into a branch of anthropology. Fine for him, but if he takes away our simplifying psychological assumption — that man seeks to maximize his gains and minimize his losses — then he will destroy economic theory itself.

BALDWIN

Then maybe it should be destroyed. If it is false, empty scholasticism, destroy it! If it has no relation to the actual functioning of the system, destroy it!

LASSITER

Revolutionary appetites, it appears, are contagious.

THAYER

My gastronomic appetite is all that concerns me at the moment.

BALDWIN

The one shudders and denounces every important new idea as revolutionary; the other concentrates upon his stomach.

THAYER

I beg your pardon?

BALDWIN

That's the agony of it: that the slaves become so timorous and
worshipful of money and prestige and power that they are shocked
and insulted when someone calls attention to the rings in their
noses!

LASSITER

If you were in my department, young man, you'd soon find out
who wears the ring in his nose!

LAUGHLIN

Herbert, don't be an ass. And I'll thank you not to intimidate
the junior members of my department.

BALDWIN

I'm scared to death!

THAYER

Where the devil is Veblen?

LAUGHLIN

I wonder if something can be wrong? He hasn't been well . . .

THAYER

[Smuttily.] Do you suppose he needs a woman's tender loving
care?

BALDWIN

Thayer, that's a dirty crack.

LAUGHLIN

You know, gentlemen, I really think it would be the best thing
all around if you all ran along and left me alone with Veblen.

THAYER

I daresay you are right. And as I am already late . . .

BALDWIN

Suits me.
  [*The professors are just getting to their feet, when* VEBLEN
  *enters. He is now forty-nine; he is wearing a woolen dress-
  ing gown and has grown a Van Dyke beard.*]

VEBLEN

I am afraid I have kept you waiting, gentlemen.

LASSITER

Indeed you have! Thayer, Baldwin and I are on our way out.
We leave you to Laughlin.

VEBLEN

[*Coldly.*] Oh? Well, good afternoon!

BALDWIN

I just want you to know . . .

VEBLEN

[*Ignoring him.*] Here, here, let me show you to the door.
  [LASSITER, THAYER *and* BALDWIN *leave.* VEBLEN *sits in an easy
  chair, affecting a very detached manner.*]

VEBLEN

Well, what's on your mind, Laurence?

LAUGHLIN

[*Moving closer to him.*] You missed one scorcher of a faculty
meeting.

VEBLEN

They decided to tear down the library and build a larger football stadium?

LAUGHLIN

This is serious, Thorstein.

VEBLEN

Am I being given to understand that the distinguished faculty of the University of Chicago saw fit to discuss the life and works of one Thorstein Bunde Veblen?

LAUGHLIN

President Harper was hot as a pistol. Have you seen the review of your book in the new International Socialist Review?

VEBLEN

I have not.

LAUGHLIN

Then listen to this; Harper read it to the faculty: "In this epoch-making volume, *The Theory of the Leisure Class*, Veblen, the revolutionary iconoclast, throws around the conventions and ethics handed down from the past with all the joyous unconcern of a bovine male in an emporium for the sale of ceramic products. And how can a socialist fail to gurgle with glee when he realizes that this bomb was constructed by a Rockefeller employee in the Standard Oil laboratories at the University of Chicago?"

VEBLEN

[*Laughs.*] I suppose someone rose to defend me on grounds of academic freedom?

LAUGHLIN

A few of us did. Things got a bit thick. The president maintained that academic freedom does not include the freedom to construct bombs. The president had his supporters.

VEBLEN

And did the learned faculty also discuss my love life?

LAUGHLIN

Not in the meeting. But it's all over the campus . . . Thorstein, I hope you don't mind my interfering, but I am determined to keep you on my staff if I can . . . I went to see Harper last night about your . . . domestic relations.

VEBLEN

That wasn't sensible, Laurence. It's not your affair — any more than it is Harper's.

LAUGHLIN

I have been trying to be realistic. You don't seem to realize how serious this is.

VEBLEN

So what did his holiness have to say?

LAUGHLIN

He offered terms. He made two stipulations: First, that Mrs. Veblen come back to you. Second, [*taking a letter out of his pocket*] that you sign this paper saying you will have no further relations with your lady-friend.

VEBLEN

Tell his majesty: First, Mrs. Veblen is welcome here but she will not come back. Second, I am not signing anything. I am not in the habit of promising to do what I have no intention of doing. I am going to resign, and that is the end of it.

LAUGHLIN

That's what he wants! Don't do it! . . . Thorstein, I've got something to tell you: Your wife is in town.

VEBLEN

[*Flushing.*] Oh? You have seen her?

LAUGHLIN

Yes, early this morning . . . As a matter of fact, I met her at the station when she got in from Utah. I'd telegraphed her about the situation. She's gone to see Harper.

VEBLEN

Laurence, why don't you learn to mind your own business? . . . I think we've said enough for one day.

LAUGHLIN

Thorstein, you can't resign. Make a fight of it!

VEBLEN

I don't need his assistant professorship.

LAUGHLIN

But what are you going to do?

VEBLEN

You underestimate me, Laurence. Stanford wants me. They'll give me a promotion. They'll double my salary. I'm taking their offer.

LAUGHLIN

Well. So you've made up your mind?

VEBLEN

I have.

LAUGHLIN

I see . . . Well, I can only offer you my congratulations, Thorstein . . . I'm glad for you, but I'm going to miss you. It seems . . . [*Breaks off.*] But you've never been one for sentiment.

VEBLEN

No. But I appreciate everything you have done, Laurence.

LAUGHLIN

I believe that.

> [*There is a knock at the door.* THORSTEIN *in agitation goes to open it.* ELLEN ROLFE *enters slowly. Her hair is white, her face sharp and strained.*]

VEBLEN

Hello, Ellen. Did you lose your key?

ELLEN

No, I have it. Hello, Professor Laughlin.

LAUGHLIN

I was just leaving, Mrs. Veblen. Will you please excuse me?

ELLEN

Of course.

VEBLEN

Goodbye, Laurence. I'll see you later. [*Exit* LAUGHLIN.] So you're back and have seen Harper?

ELLEN

Laurence told you?

VEBLEN

Ellen, listen to me, I don't want you ever to do a thing like that again! You hear me? Don't you ever do it again!

ELLEN

Never again. I'm sorry. Forgive me.

VEBLEN

Don't be sorry! Just use your head . . . What did he say?

ELLEN

He said he wasn't interested. Then I . . . I talked a lot . . . and finally he asked me if I would come back and live with you if he let it go this time.

VEBLEN

And what did *you* say?

ELLEN

I said, if it meant your staying, I would come back.

VEBLEN

Well, I am *not* staying, so you needn't have bothered! Oh, God, how humiliating! How degrading!

ELLEN

Oh, I enjoyed it, every minute of it. Never have I had such a delightful conversation . . . I wish . . . Excuse me, Thorstein [*Sits down abruptly.*] Would you mind getting me a glass of water and one of my pills? Are they there?

THORSTEIN

Of course! [*Runs out of the room, returns with water and pills.* ELLEN *throughout sits very still. Drinks the water, swallows pills.*] Ellen, what in God's name is it?

ELLEN

Nothing. A headache . . . [*Stands up.*] I'm fine. Sorry . . .

VEBLEN

Please sit down, Ellen. You're not well.

ELLEN

There is nothing wrong with me . . . Honestly . . . Well, I could have spared the trip. You are resigning . . .

VEBLEN

Yes, Ellen, I have made up my mind. And I have other news for you. I've been made a very good offer by Stanford in California. Promotion, salary doubled — what do you think of that?

Wait till we throw that in Harper's face! . . . You get a good rest and then we'll go out to California together and get settled.

ELLEN

[*Sitting down.*] You are quite mad . . . Give me five minutes and I'll be on my way.

VEBLEN

You said you would stay!

ELLEN

Please, Thorstein, please . . . You're not a child . . . [*Looks around the room.*] Very tidy! She must be a competent house-keeper.

VEBLEN

She has not been here in a week!

ELLEN

Oh, God, that is what kills me! Not that you do these things, but the way you throw them in my face!

VEBLEN

I am throwing nothing in your face. You asked me a question. I gave you an answer. Would you prefer me to become a liar in my old age?

ELLEN

You could have lived as you like, done as you like. I don't deceive myself. I know only too well that physically, emotionally, our life . . . our life . . . I can understand . . . I can see that there would be a need for these affairs. But, Thorstein, these *insults* to me I cannot stand and will not stand!

VEBLEN

Insults? What insults?

ELLEN

Oh! ! !

VEBLEN

She moved in! What was I supposed to do?

ELLEN

Not being a man, I wouldn't know the answer to that.

VEBLEN

I tell you there is no answer!

ELLEN

With you, there is never an answer. There is only what is. [*Mocks him.*] "Do not speak of what should be; speak of what is." When you went off to Europe by yourself, without even asking if I wanted to go, there was no answer. When you left me night after night to sit here alone, there was no answer. When you ignored me, insulted my friends, walked out on my parties, there was no answer. What is it? Are you so ashamed of me? Am I so offensive? Am I so ugly? Am I so much more stupid than your other friends?

VEBLEN

I never said you were stupid. Never! You have been a good companion.

ELLEN

A good companion!

VEBLEN

What is so terrible about that? Another insult?

ELLEN

Yes, yes, a terrible insult.

VEBLEN

This is hysteria.

ELLEN

Once we had a life, but you have forgotten. You have driven me out of it. You drive everything out of it. You don't want friends, you don't want students, you don't want a wife, you don't want a marriage!

VEBLEN

[*The mask coming off.*] It could have been different . . . Maybe if . . . if we had had a child . . .

ELLEN

Had a child! [*Bursts into tears.*] And what happened when I was pregnant?

VEBLEN

You were not pregnant!

ELLEN

I was! [*Relentlessly.*] What happened? [*He turns away: he doesn't want to hear this.*] You fool! What a wonderful memory! The greatest memory in the world! But this *I* remember. What did you do? Who carried on like a lunatic? Who left me for three days? Who made me so sick I could have died, should have died? Oh, God, we should have had a child! Oh, my God, my dear God! Why? Why did you do it to me? Why do you do it now? [*Sobs.*]

VEBLEN

[*Overcome.*] Ellen . . . I don't know, Ellen . . .

ELLEN

Then who knows?

VEBLEN

One of me . . . is enough . . . Ellen, Ellen, forgive me.

ELLEN

I forgive you. So let me alone. [*She gets to her feet.*] So that's done, that's over . . .

VEBLEN

You can't go. I have a responsibility . . . You are not well. You are in no condition . . .

ELLEN

I'm all right. Just tired. Just dead . . . Thorstein, believe me, I am not angry. I am past anger, past anything. Please, I just want to go.

VEBLEN

Ellen, don't ask me to beg you . . .

ELLEN

No, please don't beg me . . . Just let me alone . . . Do you mind if I take a few things with me? Some of my books?

VEBLEN

Take whatever you want.
    [ELLEN *goes to the tall bookshelf, begins pulling out some
    books and dropping them to the floor. . . .* VEBLEN *dumbly
    watches her.*]

FADE-OUT

Scene 2

Lights up on a small classroom at the University of Missouri. The time is December, 1916. In the room are six students, four boys and two girls; they have their coats over their shoulders, are leaning against the desks with hats on, restlessly. The professor's desk faces the audience.

BOY 1

He's a freak!

GIRL 1

I swear I never know what he's talking about.

BOY 1

What the hell is he going to give us for grades in here? He never reads an examination. He never gives one back.

BOY 2

M's. Everybody gets M's.

GIRL 1

I think he's nuts.

BOY 1

He lives alone like a hermit in that hole under Davenport's house.

BOY 2

He ain't fit to associate with human beings. He's been kicked out of half the colleges in the country — Chicago, Stanford . . .

BOY 1

Let's go. He never checks the attendance anyway.

BOY 3

Oh, stick around. I want to hear him today. He was just getting hot on the dolicho-blonds.

BOY 1

You stick around, apple-polisher. A lot of good it will do you! You'll get an M like the rest of us.

BOY 2

After fifteen minutes, it's a cut. We can go.

GIRL 1

It's not quite fifteen minutes yet.

BOY 1

[*Near the classroom door.*] Duck! Here he comes!

BOY 2

Christ Almighty!

[*The students jump for chairs . . . Enter* VEBLEN, *now fifty-nine. He looks pallid and sick; wears a scraggly mustache and beard. A huge woolen muffler is wrapped around his neck, a fur cap with flaps is pulled down over his ears, and heavy woolen gloves cover his hands.* VEBLEN *slouches into the room and sits at the desk, without disturbing his clothes.*]

VEBLEN

If any of you wish to keep on your wraps, it will be all right with me . . . [*Pulls off one glove, takes out large pocket watch, places it in front of him.*] I beg your pardon for arriving so late.

I shall attempt to make it up to you by making today's lecture a short one. [*Laugh from the class.*] In fact, if any of you wish to leave right now, you are free to. [*Nobody has enough nerve to leave.*] Now then, before I begin, are there any questions?

BOY 1

Are we going to have a midsemester examination?

VEBLEN

Oh, yes, I had forgotten. [*Pulls at pockets, gets out a slip of paper.*] Ah, yes. I see that the chairman of the department has scheduled an examination for this class tomorrow.

CLASS

Tomorrow! ! !

VEBLEN

Tomorrow. At 10 a.m. I will be in the classroom at the time scheduled. If any student or students show up for the examination, it will probably be so severe that you could not make a passing grade. If no students show up, all members of the class will be given an M. Are there any other questions?

BOY 3

[*Raising his hand.*] Professor Veblen . . .

VEBLEN

I am not a professor. I am a lecturer.

BOY 3

Dr. Veblen . . . yesterday in discussing the emergence of the dolicho-blonds, you used the expression "real" and "conjectural

history." Now just what relation exists between real and conjectural history?

As far as I can see, the relation is about the same as that existing
between a real horse and a saw horse. [*Laughter.* VEBLEN *appears
not to notice it.*] Any more questions? Very well, then, let me see.
[*Takes off his cap; his hair is entirely gray.*] Ah, yes, we were on
the dolicho-blonds. Now we are off the dolicho-blonds. Let us talk
about a more interesting group: the Jews. Let us talk of the Jews
and the Jewish achievement.

Now the cultural history of the Jewish people is large and rich.
From ancient times they have shown aptitude for such work as
will tax the powers of thought and imagination. Their accom-
plishments, before the Diaspora, are among the secure cultural
monuments of mankind. But these achievements of the ancient
Jews do not touch the frontiers of modern science nor fall in the
lines of modern scholarship.

It appears that the gifted Jew comes into his own as an intellectual leader in the modern world only when he escapes from the
cultural environment created and fed by the particular genius of
his own people and enters the alien gentile world. Then he finds
himself in the vanguard of modern inquiry as a result of his loss
of allegiance to his own people — or at best as a result of a divided
allegiance to the people of his origin.

[*Slowly, the lights are narrowing in on* VEBLEN. *Eventually
all we see is his face.*]

Now the first requisite for constructive work in modern science
is a skeptical frame of mind. The important pioneering work of

guidance, design and theoretical correlation requires a degree of freedom from hard-and-fast preconceptions and a release from the dead hand of conventional finality and inherited truth.

The intellectually gifted Jew is in a particularly fortunate position in respect to this requisite immunity from the dead hand of the past. But he attains such immunity only at the cost of losing his secure place in the scheme of conventions into which he was born. He must also suffer the cost of finding no secure place in that scheme of gentile conventions into which he is thrown.

For him and for all others like him, the skepticism that has made the Jew an effectual factor in the increase and spread of knowledge involves a loss of that peace of mind that is the birthright of the safe and sane quietist. He becomes a disturber of the intellectual peace, but at the cost of becoming an intellectual wayfaring man, a wanderer in the intellectual no-man's-land. He searches for another place to rest, farther along the road, somewhere over the horizon. They are not a contented lot, these aliens of the uneasy feet.

The young Jew who is gifted with a taste for knowledge unavoidably must go far afield into that area of learning where the gentile interests dominate and the gentile orientation gives the outcome.

GIRL STUDENT

[*Whispers.*] I didn't know Veblen was a Jew.

BOY STUDENT

[*Whispers.*] Don't be an idiot! He's a Norskie from Minnesota!

VEBLEN

The Jew who searches after learning must go beyond the pale of his own people. But although he finds his own heritage untenable, he does not therefore take over and assimilate the traditions of usage and outlook which the new world has to offer. The idols of his own tribe have crumbled in decay and no longer cumber the ground, but his release from them does not induce him to set up a new line of idols borrowed from an alien tribe.

Intellectually, he is likely to become an alien. Spiritually, he is more likely to remain what he was — for the heartstrings of affection are tied early and they are not readily retied in after life. Nor does the hostile reception he finds waiting for him in the community of the safe and sane make possible his personal incorporation in that community, whatever may befall the intellectual assets he brings. Their people need not become his people, nor their gods his gods. Indeed, the provocation is always present to turn back from following after them. The most amiable share in this foreign community's life that is likely to befall him is that of being interned.

One who goes away from home will come to see many unfamiliar things, and to take note of them. But it does not follow that he will swear by all the strange gods he meets along the road.

[VEBLEN *rises from the desk, comes slowly forward. In the following passage, each new character is spot-lighted and blacked-out in turn.*]

KARI

Thorstein, come back. Come back! It's not too late.

VEBLEN

I've lost the way.

KARI

You have your home; you have your God.

THORSTEIN

Mother, I can't turn back.

KARI

Stubborn fool! Admit when you're wrong!

THORSTEIN

Mother, go away.

KARI

Come with me.

THORSTEIN

What for?

KARI

To find peace, find rest.

THORSTEIN

That's simple. I'll find them soon enough.

KARI

Not you. A million years and you'll never rest! You're damned!
  [KARI *out.*]

THOMAS VEBLEN

Don't mind your mother.

THORSTEIN

I don't. She doesn't know what she's saying.

THOMAS

What makes you so sure?

THORSTEIN

I'm sure of nothing.

THOMAS

Then maybe you should try to believe?

THORSTEIN

Believe in what? In a tribal god? In the gospel according to St. Olaf? What for? Deny my life? Deny myself? Deny all that I have seen and learned? Deny the evidence of the world as it is? Cry like a baby, beg for mercy? Humble myself, lie to myself? Say Mother, Mother, forgive, forgive?

THOMAS

She wants only your happiness. That's all she's seeking.

THORSTEIN

A funny way! It always starts with love and ends with threats and curses . . . A million years I'll walk the earth! The Wandering Norwegian!

THOMAS

Sometimes there are deep truths in these stories . . .

THORSTEIN

You keep the deep truth, Father. My deep truth is that I will die and rot.

THOMAS

Your life is a misery.

THORSTEIN

Happiness belongs to the idiots.

THOMAS

You've grown so hard, Thorstein, so cruel.

THORSTEIN

Have I?

THOMAS

You were not that kind of a boy.

THORSTEIN

I was a coward when I was a boy.

THOMAS

You never were. You always fought well.

THORSTEIN

Not inside. Inside I was yellow. They hated me, and I was afraid to hate back. I've learned to hate back.

THOMAS

Unlearn it!
  [THOMAS *out*.]

THORSTEIN

[*Ironically*.] In the next life . . . surrounded by my legion of friends.

LAUGHLIN

I tried to be your friend.

THORSTEIN

You were, Laurence. You were the salt of the earth.

LAUGHLIN

You dug your own grave. If you had only observed the conventions . . .

THORSTEIN

Bowed down to the idols, you mean. I despised all the idols, old ones and new ones. I spit on them.

LAUGHLIN

You can't make the world over.

THORSTEIN

Maybe not.

LAUGHLIN

So what does it matter? Accept, pretend . . .

THORSTEIN

You'd laugh if I told you why I couldn't.

LAUGHLIN

I could use a laugh.

THORSTEIN

It would have been immoral.

LAUGHLIN

Immoral? By what brand of morality?

THORSTEIN

By the only brand I know: the morality of science. The morality that says: Don't be a liar, inside or outside. The morality that asks: What is the evidence? And then says: Spread the word!

LAUGHLIN

But a man has to live.
[LAUGHLIN *out*.]

THORSTEIN

Tell it to the world! . . . That is why I hate them: They wouldn't let me live. Except as a slave, except as a liar, they wouldn't let me live . . .

ELLEN

But what did I do to you?

THORSTEIN

Who said you did anything?

ELLEN

Then why did you hate me?

THORSTEIN

I did not hate you, Ellen.

ELLEN

You say everything backwards.

THORSTEIN

Very well . . . Then listen: I loved you and I love you. Do you hear? Are you satisfied?

ELLEN

Then what did it all mean?

THORSTEIN

How do I know?

ELLEN

Oh, tell me, tell me!

THORSTEIN

It means I stayed a coward. It means I was afraid of hatred and afraid of love.

ELLEN

And afraid of your son.

THORSTEIN

I hid from you and I hid from him. I ran and threw myself down in the field . . . That terrible running, that sinking into darkness . . . Then shame. Years and years of shame . . . One day a child came to me and said, "T. B. Veblen. What does T. B. stand for?" I said it stood for Teddy Bear. He laughed at me. All my life I wanted that kind of laughter.

CURTAIN

ALTERNATIVE LIVES

Alternative
Lives

Constance Urdang

University of Pittsburgh Press

Published by the University of Pittsburgh Press, Pittsburgh, Pa. 15260
Copyright © 1990, Constance Urdang
All rights reserved
Baker & Taylor International, London
Manufactured in the United States of America

Library of Congress Cataloging-in-Publication Data

Urdang, Constance.
   Alternative lives / Constance Urdang.
      p.   cm. — (Pitt poetry series)
   ISBN 0-8229-3650-X. — ISBN 0-8229-5439-7 (pbk.)
   I. Title. II. Series.
   PS3571.R3A79   1990
   811'.54—dc20   90-33962
                                            CIP

Some of these poems have appeared, perhaps in slightly different form, in *The First Anthology of Missouri Women Writers, New Letters, The New Republic, Ontario Review, Panoply, Ploughshares, Poetry, Poetry Review, River Styx, Shenandoah, The Southern California Anthology, Tendril,* and *Western Humanities Review.* "Emergency Ward, St. Vincent's" originally appeared in *The New Yorker.*

The publication of this book is supported by grants from the National Endowment for the Arts in Washington, D.C., a Federal agency, and the Pennsylvania Council on the Arts.

for Don, in spite of hell and transmigration

Contents

I

Contents

I

Envy of Other Lives

1. Envy of the Artist

To stand in a large, empty room, freezing cold,
Confronting the easel in the eye of a storm of light,
Your only weapon "a kitchen knife
With which to stick layers of paint
On a large, empty canvas," like Courbet
(On the mantel, a bottle and half-empty glass);
Or to be like Monet, who seized the brightness
From a cliff-face, then "plunged his hands
Into a rainstorm, and flung it onto the canvas"—
Like Klee, to live "somewhat closer to the heart
Of creation than usual;" to make a truthful image
Of the world, so that when we go to Holland
We understand everything the landscape says
Because the painters have acted as interpreters,
So that Mexico itself "seems a motif invented
By Diego Rivera;" because
The mystery of the world is in the visible,
And to stand in a large, empty room
In front of a blank canvas, equipped
With nothing but brush and pigment, is to become
An instrument through which the world's remade.

2. Envy of the Cow

Foursquare in the breathtaking landscape,
Dreamy, imperturbable, steadfastly munching,
She does not need to look at the view.
Under her mild brown liquid eye
Earth has set out a lush banquet,
Such succulent flavors and juices
Extracted from acres awash with light,
Rich fields lying tawny and fallow, violet
Distances frosted with cloud
For her to feed on, she is taking it all,

3

Ruminant mouthful by mouthful,
Sprout, sprig, and blade
Into herself. Now she nibbles away a meadow,
Swallows a hillside, devours
A wood, then a cluster of tile-roofed houses—
Even the highway finds a road
Down her omnivorous gullet, till, having taken
All of it in, the cow becomes part of the scene.

3. *Envy of Audacity*

Instead of staying in the doll corner
Playing Mother, Father, and Baby, instead
Of cooking and eating, crying and cleaning, to go
Where "the drive to live is stronger than elsewhere,"
To enter the domain of the impossible,
Where foreign tongues take on a libidinal quality
And fraud and deception reveal their dear delights;
To travel roads scarcely marked, tinged
With the faint smell of brimstone, to penetrate
Wild fastnesses where barbaric customs drown
Infant daughters in milk, or let them be trampled
To death, and Christians and Jews
Are impaled or crucified, to dare
To live the fantasies poets only imagine,
Preferring "a dry crust, privations, pain, and danger"
To a life among stiff old houses and historic markers
Where every avenue points to a known destination
And to every adventure's melancholy end.

4. *Envy of the Circus*

Drawn by the meretricious glitter
Of spangles and sequins, above
The ring's sweaty odors, its glint
Of fools' gold in the dust—

4

To welcome the real brute, danger, that plunges
With the lions into the spotlight, while frolicsome music
Makes light of powerful jaws, to join
The purposeful climb of the aerialist
To the top of the tent, to lean with him
Into the tantalizing rhythms of the trapeze
Is to know with the wire-walker that to be
On the wire is life, and the rest,
The rest, below, is nothing but waiting.

5. Envy of the Past

It's where nothing can harm you; even the painfulness
Of pain, faded like an old snapshot,
Turns emblematic. If yesterday's flowerlike faces
Have power to pierce the heart, it's only
Because we know what they did not foresee
Past the edge of the frame. In the poet's house
Years later, no tremors can still be felt,
And the sadness of old letters under glass
Awakens only an agreeable nostalgia.
Returning to the Loncheria del Ausente
Is no longer possible. Looking backward
Is the only way to experience again
The true feeling of exile.

Alternative Lives

"I could not live like a vegetable in the country."
—Isabel Burton

I could live like a vegetable in the country;
Brushing off crumbs of sleep, the rich loam of dreams,
I'd open one sly eye to the far-off, blue, indifferent sky, swell
In the dark soil, fatten under the moon,
Grow long and pale, or purple as beet, underground;
I could live earthy as a potato, or climb toward heaven
On a trellis, like these beans; why wouldn't
Such a life be sweet?
                    I can picture
Myself in a white apron, shelling peas in a dooryard,
Scattering grain for ducks, gathering eggs
Still warm from the nest. September
Would be the best time, picking apples
From gnarled trees where they'd been ripening
Secretly, in their own time, all summer long.

A Life You Might Say You Might Live

You might call it *a road*,
This track that swerves across the dry field,
And you might call this alley a *street*,
This alley that stumbles downhill between the high walls
And what you might call *doorways*, these black mouths
That open into caves you might call *houses;*
And if you turned at the corner
Into a narrower alley, you might still call it
Going home, and when you got to the place
Where it dwindles to a footpath, and you kept on walking
You would finally come to what you might call *the threshold*
Of a life, of what you might call *your life.*

The Grey Cat

How I envy Mrs. Payne and her husband
Who felt unusual throbbing sensations
A year ago at the Washington Park Zoo
In Portland, Oregon, and knew they were eavesdropping
On the secret code of elephants;
Or Dr. David Gibo, who built a hang-glider
And soared with the monarch butterflies,
Breasting the blue thermals—

For the grey cat is calling, but not to me.
From out of his own wilderness
Only his black-banded banner of a tail
Signals where he is headed under the ghost-pale moon
That, silent and alone,
Continues to sail toward California
Between the yellow flower that opens in the morning
And the *bleu lumière* of afternoon.

The Game of Troy

You want to smash the pattern of everyday,
The dailyness of it, the waking with sticky eyelids,
Feet finding the floor, the toothbrush finding the teeth,
Cold water, then warmer, in the inevitable shower
You don't even remember stepping into, shirt, socks, and so on,
Stairs—and the cat in, or out—
The same thing every day, the same sun
Glinting on fenders and chrome of Fords and Toyotas,
All over the city, people rushing to work with ham sandwiches
Monday to Friday, and weekends at the lake—
Do you think it was different in an age of heroes?
That every day had its dragon? Even on the plain of Troy
Achilles sulked in his tent, and after the fighting was over
Helen would probably have been glad
To go back and be a common housewife.
As for Odysseus, that cunning dawdler,
He invented his own adventures, or Homer did,
Telling tall tales, taking the long way home.

Water Intoxication

Fatherless women who thirst in secret
Have been know to use all the water in the house
Mopping and scrubbing, lunatic laundresses,
Pouring whatever is left down the drain
Or flinging it out the door in a silvery flood
To leave themselves high and dry through another night.

But O in the dewy morning they wake awash
In a watery world, standing all day
Open-mouthed in the shower, or stationed
All day at the drinking fountain, because for them
Water is truly the serum transfusion of life,
Because woman is created out of water.

When a huge wave crashes at their feet
They carefully gather the fragments together
And husband the glittering shards in their cupped hands
And throw them, flashing, back into the ocean,
Mother of waters, and mother of fatherless women.

Robert's Knee

Robert who, more than anyone, abhors
Superstition, and things that can't be explained,
In Manila consulted a psychic surgeon for his knee.
It was in the interest of science.
The house was far out in the suburbs, a long ride
In a rattletrap taxi, with doors wired to close
Like the ones kidnappers use, and upholstery cracked open
To ooze an ambiguous stuffing.

I imagine a house of painted pink stucco.
I imagine a weedy yard with a rusty gate.
I imagine a small, hot room. A single naked bulb
Sways on a cord above the table. I imagine
A woman in a sweaty flowered dress
Welcoming, wearing gold-rimmed glasses. The surgeon enters;
He is a cousin of the taxi driver, small, serious,
In a business suit. He washes his hands at the sink
As the woman positions Robert on the table.
I cannot imagine what will happen next.

It takes a long time. Robert's knee has been examined
By doctors in Denver, St. Louis, and Washington, D.C.
They have attacked it with scalpels and forceps,
They have manipulated it with trained fingers,
They have introduced, through a microscopic incision,
The most advanced instruments, and prescribed
A regimen using pulleys and weights—
Now the surgeon is rubbing his hands over Robert's knee.
It glistens with oil and salve, but Robert can't see it.
Where he lies he can only watch the woman
As she right now touches a match to a single stick
Of incense, and into the corners of the room
Creeps a thin, blue, pungent thread. There is no pain
In the knee, or anywhere, when suddenly
The surgeon raises, with a grunt, a bloody hand
Squeezing something that oozes, something like grit or sand,

And displays it to Robert before he flings it, *splat!*
Into a basin. That's it, then.
                                    I imagine
Robert sitting up to examine his knee.
It looks the same. There is no incision;
This surgeon does not cut. Since flesh is grass,
It moves aside to let him reach within
And pluck out what offends. He's pleased,
Washing his hands. The woman takes the money.

Next morning Robert wonders if he feels
A brief returning twinge. He can't be sure.

Silvino

Silvino, who promised to be here early
To fix the light switches and install the washtubs,
Instead is scurrying through the town
Searching for switchplates and wire, washers and screws
He knew last week he'd need for the job.
I see him skittering from Vulcan to Esmeralda;
There's a shortage of switchplates. Maybe tomorrow
Or maybe next week, or maybe
In another town, he'll find them. Unpredictably now
These shortages: last month it was toothpaste,
In April, milk. From the shelves in the little shops
Detergents vanish, then cooking oil. Silvino is running
Faster now, he's sweating. At home, too many babies.
When he comes empty handed, his wife blames him.
Not long ago he came courting with hair slicked down,
His arms blossoming with roses and carnations.

Carmen

Carmen asks if it is cold, now, in my country.
She wants to know how far it is to where I live.
She wonders if the people there have work,
If they have money, if they have toothache.
Is it a hard journey?
Would it be possible for her to go there?

There are no words for what I have to tell her:
There is no road for her to where I live.
The bridges are all washed out, the highways flooded;
Even in blistering heat my country is cold.
The people have barred their doors against her children,
And there is no room for her at their tables.

Mrs. Mandrell and the Water Table

On the day the well ran dry
Mrs. Mandrell bathed in soda water
Icy and scentless as the mountain spring
Where it erupted and was bottled
Then trucked to her where she lay.

Did its barrage of bubbles
Prickle against her skin?
Did she fizz all over like imported champagne?
Did her body become strange to her,
Suspended in Perrier water?

Luminous in crystal, her body is immortal
In a thousand museums and galleries,
But Mrs. Mandrell is not a renewable resource.
Being writ on water, ambiguous element
From which life springs, when all the wells run dry,
With what shall she be watered?

Frida and I

Following a freak accident that impaled her on a steel rod and doomed
her to a life of pain, Frida Kahlo (1907–1954) became a painter.

Walking into my life one morning on Riverside Drive
With no idea of what to expect, how could I have foreseen
Maguey with tall stalks like giant asparagus
Exploded at the tip into bonsai shapes
Like the windswept pines of northern California,
Or these seminal pigments, crude primary yellows,
Magenta of bougainvillaea, scarlet and vermilion,
Acidic olive greens, puke greens, pinks, purples,
Green-bronze, nut brown, cinnamon, that exhale
An acrid smoke into the thin blue air?
                                 In a black doorway
A girl teeters on spike heels, waiting for her life.
She can't imagine how it will arrange itself
Or what it will offer her. Frida never saw
The accident that created her, changing her in an instant
That never ended, into art. Below the scaffold
Where Rivera painted, she came with her basket, *folklorico*,
Or lay immured in plaster, her screams translated
Into paint, *Frida* after *Frida*, a procession
Whose heroine was death, "little aunt of the little girls."

Death is no stranger in Mexico,
Whether in the blue house on Londres Street
Or in the square near the university
Or in the room never mentioned, behind the police station.
Even in New York it followed her
Through the open window of Hampshire House
Three giant steps down to the sidewalk, as she painted it.

In Paris, she had appetite for the food
But none for the French, and returned inevitably
To the land of the prickly pear, spiny fruit of Mexico
In a parade of self-portraits. They bleed not only
For Frida, but for all she knew, sisters and brothers
Pierced by the thorns of history,
Struggling in violent times to make a life.
Every poem is a self-portrait.

A Little Elegy

for Miriam

1.

When she left, it was without the customary preparations.
The house was in a curious disorder;
No trunks were packed, the dishes left from breakfast
Still stood on the table, and in the upstairs bedrooms
Beds yawned in dismay. How unlike her it was
To embark on such a long journey without making all the
arrangements,
Storing away the things that would not be needed
In closets and attics, everything in its place.
She is gone taking nothing, without saying goodbye,
Leaving in the house an emptiness
That will not be filled.

2.

I thought I would make a wreath
Of the dark green leaves of the homely little plants
She tended with such faithfulness,
Interwoven with mysterious messages, overgrown with the moss
Of old German fairy tales,
Hung with the volatile syllables
Of the French language, strung
With lighthearted ribbons of the baroque,
Music of hautboy, viola da gamba, continuo.
But, clumsy-fingered, I only have these words
To hang on the empty air.

3.

She was one with the mothers
Whose children have disappeared. She was one with those
Who come carrying in a single bundle
All they have in the world, across invisible frontiers.
She stood alone, like a tree
Which is always alone, even when it is surrounded
By other trees. She wept alone in her room.

4.

Let rain be her requiem.
The steady unemphatic drizzle
That drenched the mourners on the pale hillside
Where they lowered her ashes into the sodden earth;
The monotone of the dull rains of December;
Crescendo of an equinoctial storm;
Soft summer showers, that sigh the night away
In the garden abandoned beyond weeping windows.

Magritte and the American Wife

In the artist's studio she was amazed
To find furniture such as you might see
In any bourgeois apartment.
A patterned carpet, and curtains at the windows;
The artist himself, "tightly buttoned
Into a dark business suit,"
Thick, rather than fat, short, middle-aged,
Fit disappointingly into his surroundings.
Only the spotless easel betrayed him.

When she asked if he didn't
Get paint on the carpet, he told her he applied
The paint to the canvas, having thought out
In advance, where he would put it.
It was only then she noticed, growing
On a prim Victorian chair,
A lion's tail, and, concealed
In the domestic architecture,
The naked glowing torso of a woman.

Robert's Friends

A host of invisible presences, they are everywhere,
Robert's friends, swarming like gnats
Or shrinking into corners
Like dust mice that have escaped the broom;
When you least expect it you might stumble over one
On the stair, or surprise them in your room.
The air is full of their voices, a muttering descant
Not unlike the speech of elephants, "resembling
The vibrations from the lowest note
On a big pipe-organ, or the slight shock wave
From far-off thunder," something felt
Rather than heard. When Robert leaves,
A palpable absence swells in the house,
As if a glittering procession had just passed there,
A parade with floats and drum majorettes and bands,
Leaving only the echo of trumpets and marching feet
And a barely perceptible troubling of the air.

For the Girl They Tease with the Name "Lizard"

My love, my loving, my lizard-girl,
Beautiful and strange as a lizard,
Fragile, scale perfect in detail,
Fire-breathing, quicksilver-quick
As a lizard,
Which is a dragon in miniature,
Which swiftly climbs the wall on soundless feet,
Which stretches itself in the sun,
Which vanishes into the wall in search of darkness,
Consider how many monkish imaginations,
My lively, my lovely, my jewel-eyed,
Cloisonné-mailed, cloth of gold,
Field of a thousand flowers,
Lizard, you have illuminated.

Son

It is fitting for the son
To go out searching,
To look for his life
Along treeless interstates,
In dull industrial cities,
In towns sucked dry by the wind
And circled by farms
Called Stony, Bleak, Hungry, Desolation;
He thinks of a hillside pasture
Under the rain.
He thinks of pitching a tent
Near an inland stream.
He thinks of piano bars
And little cafés
Under striped awnings,
And sleek acquiescent girls.
He thinks of having everything,
And of the freedom of having nothing.
He will be a millionaire
At twenty-five.
He will put on a tie
And be punctual.
He will be a man.
He will walk up the street hatless
Thinking about his life.
He will wonder
If this is what he meant.
Now he holds the clues
In his hand, a cryptogram
He can't decipher.

My Father's Death

He knew it was waiting for him   somewhere
His own death   that he had sailed to meet
Years ago in Flanders   he never spoke
Of that broken appointment
But throughout the years that followed
He looked for it   among the frail shells
On the beaches of Maine and Connecticut
Or in the pages he loved   of books heady with mildew
Sometimes he forgot it
Till it nipped at his leg   almost playfully
Where the shrapnel still festered
When he was a boy, weak-eyed   in long black stockings
He heard its voice in the sound of milk carts
Grumbling over the cobbles   in his mother's breathy sighs
In the clatter of the el trundling over the points   later
He thought he had outfaced it at the Polyclinic
But he still had a thousand miles to go
To find it   reaching out to take my hand
His own grew cold   and stiffened in the clasp
Of the inevitable last embrace

On Rereading the Poets

Thinking about the mad poets,
The drunken, the drugged, the dead poets,
The forgotten ones, those half-remembered
For badly remembered lines, misunderstood,
Admired for the wrong reasons, and too late,
I am amazed at the persistence of poetry.

Like the secret writing of children
That becomes visible on paper held over a flame,
Obstinately, the old lines come to life
Letter by letter, stuttering across the page,
Confounding criticism, fanned into breath
Over and over, making themselves new again.

This Poem

If you are cold, this poem will not warm you.
If you are hungry, you will not be fed
By this poem; if you are sick
It will not cure you. If you are alone
The poem won't take your hand.

This poem lives in warm houses;
It has never known hunger. All it can do
Is, from a pocket of loose change
Select a coin to drop into your palm,
The cold coin of compassion in this poem.

The Apparition

When the head of Jesus appeared on the bathroom door
Nobody wanted to believe it, but there it was,
Gradually developing like a bad negative,
Those flowing locks, those deep, compassionate eyes
Darkening on the plain wood of the door
Where nothing but the grain of the cheap pine
Had been visible before.

This happened in an ordinary house
Built about eighty years ago, by a man
Who built several others in the neighborhood.
All of them are still lived in, but of course
There have been changes—though in none
Had any kind of apparition
Ever been seen before.

Since no one reported it, nobody came
To kiss it or chip holy splinters off the door,
Or wait for it to weep miraculous tears
And cure cancer or reverse a fatal course;
In any case, it would have been too late
To save my friend, who died suddenly last year
Not having been ill before.

Four Ways to Spend an Evening

1. Sending an Invitation to the Muse

There's no one here; see, we could be alone
In an ambiance of—what did he call it?
Luxe, calme, et volupté—or, if that's too French,
Let's just say I'll provide the place and time.

The place: a high white room all glass and sky
A cube of brightness glowing amid the stars,
Aladdin's cave of marvels in the air,
All richnesses and wonders. You and I

Alone would share the secrets of a time
Outside of time, where no clocks bleat the hour
Or signal starts and stops, or ever change
One season for another less condign.

Apollo, Muse, whatever name you like,
Come soon, outrun the slow horses of the night.

2. Observing the Motion of the Planets

You and I alone have considered the heavenly bodies,
Naming the constellations *scorpion, lion, bull,*
And charting their movements; these clear nights
No special equipment is needed
To pursue their imaginary paths, or study the life
Of a star, mysterious and mathematical
In the far wastes of space. Navigating
As the night birds do on their long journeys, tonight
Let us follow the apparition of Venus
And the slow declination of Mars
Which will reach opposition in September
When it is low in the east at dusk, and visible
All the long night long, to wakeful lovers.

3. Diverting the Company with Games and Music

Generally speaking, it is easier to lose
Than to win, or so it says
In the book of hard-to-follow directions. However,
The only way to play
Is to plan on winning. White sits here,
Black there. The first move
Is determined by chance
(If there is any dispute
Over who will be Black and who White,
That too will be decided
By a throw of the dice).
Following that, it is necessary only
Always to keep the odds in mind.

Luck plays a minor part
According to the book,
Like the troubling little theme
That now and then intrudes on the serene
Progress of the concerto—Mozart's Fifth
For orchestra and piano. One bad move
Is all you need, to lose.

4. Listening to the Voices in the Rain

If a woman walks past, black-shawled,
No figure of antiquity, but worn,
Her face pitted with grief,
Hers is the voice in the rain, whispering
In a language for which we have no words.

What begins as a murmur, barely distinguished
From the gossip of the wind in the leaves
That hints at much more than it ever tells,
Becomes a veritable oration, then an oratorio
For hundreds of voices, solo, duet, and chorus.

Now crescendo, now forte, staccato, diminuendo,
As if numberless black-shawled women have given tongue
In the rain that thrums all night among the leaves
To counterpoint the plainsong of their lives
That comes to us in echoes, if we listen.

The Other One

It's possible the other one's left-handed;
I've often suspected it. How else explain
A certain characteristic clumsiness,
An awkwardness that seems willful, as if determined
Not to perform, with a series of smooth gestures,
In the expected role, but instead to be gauche,
Louche as a wildling, unkempt, undomestic?

The other one's an orphan, no father or mother;
The other one's savage, not stopping to cook the meat,
But tearing it from the bones,
Ready to bed on straw, or leaves, or stones,
With any passing stranger, or with no one.

Unwelcome as a gypsy in a green wagon
Set down on the rubbishy rim of the world;
Not caring to be understood, or misunderstood,
Unblushing, unsexed, capricious as the weather;
Yes, probably left-handed.

Keats

Tomorrow I'll sit out with the poets
On our hard chairs
And let them sing their songs of despair and consolation
Into my left ear

I'll listen to them
Recite sad histories, their brave syllables
Echoing in my right ear

Sitting between
The philosophy of the porch and the
Sophistry of the garden, I'll understand
It isn't Keats I love, but the incorruptible
Purity of his words

I can let that clear flood wash over me
Like a fast-flowing stream over stones
Or lose myself in the luminous eye
Of a single stone, diving into its bottomless depths

II

Traveling Without a Camera

Imagine traveling without a camera.
How difficult it is, trying to remember
Precisely, the pattern stamped by the toothy ridges
At Real de Catorce, against an apricot sky,
Or the look of the mountainside as night overtakes it,
Reclaims it, and salts it with stars—
Which after all are not stars, but the lamps of home
To strangers you never saw and will never meet;
Or to conjure up, to what they call the mind's eye,
The exact configuration of this wall,
Weathered and crumbling, into which a lizard,
Mysteriously, vanishes.
                              Isn't this the way
You traveled through childhood, retaining only
Certain images that at first seem clear
And real as this morning, until you peer
More closely, and they disappear? Deceitful memory!
Fades and dissolves in all around I see,
As if an inept cameraman were to film
Ineptly, for a thousand thousand days,
And leave a darkroom filled with damaged prints.

Ways of Returning

Returning through the back streets, through alleys so narrow
The walls of the houses part like grass,
Leaning backward, their patience demonstrated
By scarred plaster, worm-eaten sills, and
Thrust through a chalk-blue door,
A clenched brass fist, everything the same
As it was, the sun, boys shooting marbles the same,
The same flies buzzing minarets of garbage, the same fists;
Or skating across the enormous mirrored spaces
Of an airport, in St. Louis or anywhere,
Passing the snack bars, the Budget Rent-a-Car, electronic games,
Seeing the men and women queued up to telephone
To say to someone, to anyone
At the end of the line, Hello, it's me,
I'm back; or, after driving all day long
To come into town at nightfall, the avenues
Festooned with lights, every block so familiar
You catch a glimpse of yourself coming down the street,
Yourself, in a coat you wore then, carrying something
You carried then, or maybe are carrying still.

Mornings in Mexico

The sun behind a cloud, the moon behind a tree;
On the speckled pavement
A lizard scurries without sound
And waits, with inexhaustible patience.

Here is a spray of butterflies,
A trembling mosaic of wings:
Take it, take it. Nearby
Invisible as the air, a bird is singing.

This is no time for brooding over old wrongs;
Sighs, sighs—what a wearisome litany.
See where the plain is crisscrossed with goat tracks
All the way to the twilight-colored mountains.

The Blue Door

Think of the sea as a lover,
A single salt kiss dragging you
Through monotonous green depths,
Or the sky, that the child paints
As a strip of blue at the top of the paper
When all around you in the blooming
Buzzing confusion a painting
Is waiting, or a poem:
"Some pomegranates broken open on a plate,"
One battered shoe, a tangle
Of wire coat hangers dangling from a nail,
And suddenly something wants you
To walk down this street
To the house with the blue door
And stand patiently waiting for it to open,
Confident that it will open.

The Gate

Here is the gate,
Maybe not as you imagined it;
Not an ornate affair of painted iron
Offering a tantalizing view
Between tall, welcoming pillars.
No, this gate stands like a barrier across the road,
Bland, imperturbable, indifferent,
It refuses a glimpse of what lies beyond.
It does not want to let you in.
Maybe it conceals a wilderness
Of weeds and rubble. Maybe
A broken fountain, drooling a thin thread
Of water from its cracked lip.
Maybe a sudden surge of hummingbirds,
A flight of butterflies rising on golden wings.
The gate protects its secrets.
There will always be those
Who prefer a walled garden
To a public park full of peonies and roses.

The River

Even here we have driven the river underground;
Not because we didn't admire its icy clarity,
Like glass, that scarcely bent the light of the sun;
Or because we didn't want to refresh ourselves
At its bubbling fountain,
Or bathe in it, where it purled over the stones
Singing to itself its endless song;
Not because it didn't water the plain
And carry off our refuse, washing away
The traces of our picnic on the planet;
I have seen it race like a black torrent
Down the steep channel of the street.
I have heard it roaring under the rain,
And searched for it through the dry days, hoping
For a token to show it would return.
But now it is buried under paving stones,
Deep in the rocks from which it sprang.
In the darkness it hisses and mutters, feeling its way
Like a blind man on an unfamiliar street
Tapping his path between strangers.

Instead

When the pattern changes, instead of a porcelain blue sky,
A sky like a thick woollen blanket. Instead
Of shadows with crisp black edges,
A flimsy grey veil. For "brown, dry, hard,"
Read "green." For "thirsty," read, "flowers."
When the sun emerges it is as a shy young girl
Peering from behind a curtain.
The peach tree offers a basket of fruit.
Splinters of glass in the rubbish heap
Glisten like dew, like diamonds, like
The first morning of the world.

This Life

Here we live mostly outdoors, even in the rainy season;
What is more delicious than the taste of a single raindrop
                                    on the tongue,
Or lovelier than raindrops inscribing their perfect circles
                                    in the fountain,
Or more musical than the little fugitive airs
Rain plays on the flagstones or the leaves?

Here there are houses like caves. A woman like me
Lives in a house dug out of the hillside. All day
She stoops over a smoky fire, or bends to her washing;
At night she reads poetry (spelling out each word
With a laborious finger)—I said she is like me.

Here nothing is welcoming or soft. Along the road
Other women sell creatures in paper boxes, or spiny fruit
Gathered from trees full of thorns, and the sunlight is harsh
Like the land, and the people go with masked faces
To the market, and back to their dark small houses.

What is there here to love? In winter the wells run dry
And the square overflows with tourists. Night after night
The town lights a conflagration against the darkness,
Darkness that surrounds us and would like to swallow us
As if we did not live here, as if we had never lived here.

Green Study in a Dry Climate

I am ashamed at having forgotten the name
Of this plant with its showy crimson blossoms
And shiny leaves, its stiff brown arms extended
So trustingly; I chose her myself
From among all the others, standing like orphans,
Their poor feet wedged into kerosene tins,
Beseeching faces turned toward the sun;
I took her home and fed her,
Put her on a pedestal—and she is still blooming,
But I don't remember her name.

※

And this cactus: wouldn't he protect me from my enemies?
With his clublike arms, his stubby elbows and knees,
His blunt green fists upraised, each one a bludgeon,
Wouldn't he ward off attackers? Tall as two men,
His thorny bulk bestrides the flagstones, a thousand spikes
Poised to impale. In the embrace
Of those spiny tentacles, this sentinel
Could clasp a dozen malefactors, bad men worse
Than the ones in the sad jail
Who twice a day are marched out to look at the sky
Before going back into puke-smelling cubicles
For another night of darkness and bad dreams.

※

It's clear one of the old gods
Has come to perch in the mesquite,
Having assumed the shape of a boat-tailed grackle.
He is admonishing me in a language

I don't understand, his peremptory voice
All rattles and squeals.
As the garden fills with the scent of burning
From some ancient sacrifice
I hope it is pleasing to him, his silhouette
Against the sky is so black, sharp, and imperious.

❋

I have agreed to love this poinsettia, even
When she is not in bloom, through the long months
When she offers me only a tangle
Of madder-tinted leaves. I won't imprison her
In a dark cellar, or hide her in a closet
Like some miserable Kaspar Hauser, to force her
To flower; even when she is not beautiful
I will keep her beside me,
Her downward-pointing leaves with their five sad points,
Her lugubrious brown stalks, until one day
Once more she presents me with her single outrageous blossom.

❋

What I need is a garden advisor,
An old man wise in vegetable ways
Who calls the plants by name, and talks with them; I need
Someone who knows when the moon
Is ripe for planting, I need a guide
Through this jungle I've stumbled into
By luck and love, this overgrown Eden, this intemperate land.

Salt Dreams

Here, the long growing season means slow starts.
Fresh water spills over the dam, and a hard rain drums,
Pounding, on the roof, and springs out of the waterspouts
Till the clouds are wrung dry in the strong wrists of the air.
If air were my element, I'd float in it
Like the egrets, who lift themselves clear of the heavy earth
On enormous wings spread like sails to catch the wind
That blows a salty breath from the distant ocean.

Far from salt water, I call up the gray-blue Atlantic,
Its attack and retreat on the shore, its crashing
Even when no one is there to see it or hear it,
On the black seaweedy rocks, like a froth of marble,
Its slowly gathering swells, its gathering power
Under a surface deceptive and smooth as a mirror,
Its rollers and breakers, its glittering little crests,
White horses leaping under the whip of sudden squalls.

Salt seasons the little dooryard gardens back there,
Crowded with old-fashioned blossoms of hollyhock,
Marigold, zinnia, cosmos, petunia, lily,
Commoners all, jostling one another
To their clamshell borders; it was salt on the wind
That called the little mermaid back to the sea
That never waits or is still for anyone,
And offers neither caresses nor consolation.

The Salt Museum

In the Salt Museum
Every sculpture, every carved artifact
From the massive heads and torsos
Of giants and giantesses
To antique pieces of furniture
And the most delicate
Filigrees, even fabrics
As fine as cobwebs
Is confected of salt

Here come the visitors, weeping
Wives without husbands, children
Crying for their mothers, lovers
Left lonely, to water with their tears
The displays in the Salt Museum

Each glistening teardrop, evaporated
In the museum's dry air
Deposits an infinitesimal film
On the masterpieces
In the galleries of salt

Winter Gardens (1)

Here is a little garden under glass—
Its mosses like tiny trees, its delicate ferns,
Its pebbles carpeted in lichen velvet,
Even the red-and-black Japanese bridge
That curved from nowhere to nowhere
And the flat, gray-speckled rock by the mirror pond
And the spotted salamander who lived there—
We made it years ago, without a thought
For what might lie over the curve of the bridge
In the mazy future, but took the salamander
Back to the wood to live under a root
In the odor of damp twigs and leaf mold.

Winter Gardens (2)

Everyone knows there are countries
Where winter never comes
Where language has no word for winter

In that eternal April blossoms spring up
Urgently.out of the passive soil
To embroider the air with exotic aromas

On a sunny wall
A lizard waits as patient as a stone
No harsh winds steal leaves from those trees

In those countries the seasons change
Only from oleander to hibiscus
From mango to pomegranate

While here Persephone retreats
To the darkness underground
And in winter gardens earth dreams of April

Winter Gardens (3)

When this garden was made to flower under glass
Nobody thought to set out a breakfast buffet
Where now ladies in flowery scarves
Anticipate the season
Picking and choosing among delicacies

If outside the ground is frozen hard
And beggarly December taps on the cold glass
Under the lights heat rises
From the little flames below chafing dishes
For ladies blooming in the unseasonable garden.

Pete and the Drunkards

If he had boarded the bus
With its cracked seats of imitation leather,
Keeping in his hand the flimsy ticket
For which he had paid eighty-five cents American—
That ticket with its meaningless mysterious numbers—
Couldn't Pete have stepped off into this dusty square
With its six withered trees and eight benches?
Couldn't he have walked up this alley
And rented a room in one of these small houses
Where he could unpack his satchel on the thin mattress
And leave his book on the wooden table?
Then under Mexican trees rattling in the wind,
Distraite, waving their wild green arms,
He would have found his way to a lighted doorway
And reeled with the drunkards down passages of stars,
Adrift in the Milky Way, three thousand miles from home.

At Frank 'n' Helen's

It's Nostalgia Week at Frank 'n' Helen's:
The two cops at the table near the door
Ordering pepperoni pizza have hung up
Their two blue coats, and on their brawny thighs
Their blunt black holsters dream. Under tinsel stars
Left over from Christmas, a party of seven,
Every one a senior citizen,
Is making itself at home. Over baskets
Of steaming fried chicken or shrimp
Carried by waitresses gently perspiring,
Sweethearts and strangers catch one another's eye.

Here, in the odor of down-home hospitality
Dispensed for a price (but reasonable),
America rediscovers itself, all the homely virtues
Displayed in the mirrors behind the booths
Where time has been arrested, and everything
Remains what we recall, as Frank—or Helen—
Dreamed it. Here we are all fed, we can all
Love one another. Let the scarlet hearts
Festoon the ceiling, let the walls leaf out
With mammoth cardboard shamrocks, greener far
Than anything in nature, under the dreaming stars.

The Old Ladies of Amsterdam

Indomitable, in black stockings, the old ladies of Amsterdam
Are pedaling their bicycles on the way to market.
Returning, with a chicken and some radishes,
How neatly they thread through the traffic,
Skillfully weaving in and out,
Dark figures in a sunlit tapestry.

Here are the canals of Amsterdam:
Green, sluggish, and redolent of gasoline.
It is raining on the canals. In January
They freeze. From across the Atlantic I see
The old ladies of Amsterdam balancing on silver skates,
Their black skirts whipping around their knees.

I think I am with them. Haven't I felt
A punishing wind bruise the afternoon
On a deserted block that had not been imagined
When Amsterdam was old? Behind an apartment window
An old lady is pouring pale tea from a Delft pot
In the honey-colored light of Vermeer.

Paris

Forty years later she is still the girl
Who lusted after Paris from the Left Bank,
And called from Montmartre,
Where is Paris?
The boulevards did not convince her;
Those French men and women
Marched like a scene from a film,
Black-and-white, moving unevenly,
A little grainy.
In no bistro, in no metro station
Was the true nature of Paris revealed to her.
It was not in the red geraniums
On the balcony of an apartment
Whose dark windows opened on a mysterious life.
It was not in the medieval alleys
Stinking of ancient urine,
Or in the grand hotels;
Not in the museums,
Not in the soft French sky.
Would it have been the same
To have stayed home in Manhattan, dreaming
Of entering a painting by Utrillo
Or a photograph by Cartier-Bresson?

Emergency Ward, St. Vincent's

I think they have brought me by mistake
To the Charity Bird's Hospital in Old Delhi
To be cared for like a wounded pigeon or chicken
Or to the infirmary in Morocco
Where they treat injured storks

I am lying here looking up at the yellow ceiling
At the sweating walls, and down at the tiled floor
In the cubicle next to mine something is moaning
A tough old bird is wheeled in on a gurney
And hidden behind a curtain

Now looking up I see a border of faces
Intent on a part of me beyond my view
They are nodding and muttering to one another
Poets have died before in this drafty ward
Among the diseased and the damaged

Outside in the street a purple dusk is falling
Someone is waiting in the cold corridor
For news of the accident (there is no news)
I could cry out, but instead I lie here suspended
Waiting for pain, for the reappearance of pain

Visiting the Ruins

There are ruins everywhere, both
The old romantic kind, thrusting up
Out of a mist-shrouded German lake
Or those heaps of glass and rubble in Beirut,
Garbage rotting on the avenues of Manhattan,
That don't stand for anything;

A hundred years from now they will all be one
With the buried cities of Troy, the way
Nobody now remembers the war in Spain,
And in the *Book of Compassion and Despair*
Nothing remains but scenes of sorrow and joy
Commemorated like historic sites.

So something's to be said for staying home
And reading Apollinaire in St. Louis
For translating Baudelaire in Iowa City
And looking for Rabelais in secondhand bookshops
Below Fourteenth Street
Without putting a *moi* in every landscape.

Returning to the Port of Authority:
A Picaresque

Some New Yorkers refer to the Port Authority Building, where
all buses enter and leave New York, as the "Port of Authority."

1.

Where are they going, the crowds that pass in the street?
I had not thought life had undone so many,
So many men and women, seeking the Port of Authority,
Safe anchorage, harbor, asylum.
                                    Late at night
Theirs are the voices on the radio, asking the hard questions;
Or they don't ask. The homeless, the hunted,
The haunted, the night-watchers
Who can't wait any longer for morning, where are they going?

2.

Returning, revenant, I see Eighth Avenue is a poem,
Seventh and Broadway are epics, Fifth an extravaganza
From the winos and freaks at its feet in Washington Square
(Past once-white buildings, long-ago sidewalk cafés
Behind grimy privet, Fourteenth Street's brash interruption)
To the crossover at Twenty-third.
                                    At Thirty-fourth
The mammoth parade of department stores begins,
And, on the pavement, a cacophony of hawkers
That stretches beyond the stone lions, the bravura
Of Forty-second, to a kind of apotheosis
At Fifty-ninth.
                    O prevalence of pinnacles!
O persistence of uniformed doormen sounding, in the rain,
Your lordly whistles! On Madison and Third
I am assaulted by florists' windows
Bursting with tropical blooms, I'm magnetized
By the windows of jewelry shops, by vegetables

Displayed like jewels, I'm buffeted
By the turbulence of this stream
Of life, this lyric, this mystery,
This daily miracle-play.

3.

What impossible collaborations
Are being consummated in cloud-high offices!
How many sweaty love-acrobatics are being performed
Behind a thousand windows
In the tall imperturbable hotels!
                              And all day long
The restless crowds continue in the street,
Ebbing and flowing like the tidal rivers,
And I am carried, flotsam like the rest,
Riding the crest of the flood down to the sea.

4.

Certain images I take with me,
Rescuing them from the flood;
Cast ashore, like so many others,
In a landscape I never imagined
But have come to recognize
I need something to define my life.

Coming back to the narrow island
Between the two rivers, on my right
The sweet river of memory,
And on my left the sweet river
Of forgetfulness, I see what I have become,
A woman in a blue dress,
Carried along on my own tides.

5.

Wherever I go, the river accompanies me;
It flows through my earliest dreams, its satiny surface
Fretted with lyrical little waves, or garnished
In winter, with baroque islands of ice.
Alongside, on the windswept upper deck
Of a bus, I rode to womanhood.
Now, around countless corners, in drafty offices,
Gleaming lobbies, or decorous apartments
Suspended in midair like the fabulous hanging
Gardens, I breathe its breath, and feel
Its salty undertow, tugging me home.

Calling the Nine Proud Walkers

There is no longer anyone who listens.
The voices are too insistent, there are too many
Clamoring to be heard, too many shouting,
Crying out, howling, bawling, and bellowing,
Too many mutterers, mumblers, stammerers,
Ranters and declaimers, tub-thumpers, spouters,
Incoherent babblers, gibberers, jabberers—
The wires are buzzing like an angry hive,
The airwaves, overloaded, can't transmit any more.

Silent, solitary in the starless night
I am besieged by invisible regiments,
The clamorous armies of the have-nothings.
Where are the nine proud walkers
Who might have smoothed this discord into song?

The Creation

I see him up there; he has turned his back on the world;
Hunched over the drawing-board, he is making it new
All over again, every day
The same old story, starting over
From the beginning. First, of course, the garden.

His concentration is absolute, he is inventing
Broccolis, squashes, tomatoes, pumpkins, and peas,
Green Goliaths, Early Beauties, Sweet Mamas, Jade Crosses,
And the rain that will water them, and the sun
That will shine down on them.

When he looks up, I know we see the same bird
Silhouetted against a backdrop of bristling mountains—
Not gentle little hills like sheep in a meadow—
A single bird, flashing at the tip of a twig
Like a tiny flame, like a flickering tongue of fire,

And he is inventing fire: under his pencil
Now lightning stabs the horizon, and thunder rumbles
Out of the distant mountains over the plain
Where the heavy clouds of his imagination
Perpetually ripen, pregnant with mystery.

Notes

Page 3: "a kitchen knife . . ." and "plunged his hands . . ." are translations of what de Maupassant wrote about Courbet and Monet, quoted in *The Lost World of the Impressionists*, by Alice Bellony-Rewald. Mexico "seems a motif . . ." is from *Frida: A Biography of Frida Kahlo*, by Hayden Herrera.

Page 4: "the drive to live . . ." and "a dry crust . . ." are from *The Devil Drives*, by Fawn M. Brodie.

Page 5: The wire-walker quoted is Karl Wallenda, who was killed in a fall from the high wire in 1978.

Page 8: Mr. and Mrs. Payne and the elephants were in a *New York Times* article, 11 February 1986. Dr. Gibo was in *Travel/Vistas*, 10 November 1985.

Page 10: "lunatic laundresses" from *The Female Malady*, by Elaine Showalter.

Page 21: "resembling the vibrations . . ." is from a newspaper article on earthquakes.

About the Author

Constance Urdang was born in New York City. She has a BA from Smith College and an MFA from the University of Iowa. She is the author of eight volumes of poetry and fiction, including *The Lone Woman and Others* and *Only the World*, both published in the Pitt Poetry Series. Among her awards is a National Endowment for the Arts Poetry Fellowship and the Delmore Schwartz Memorial Poetry Award. She divides her year between St. Louis, Missouri, and San Miguel de Allende, Mexico.

PITT POETRY SERIES

Ed Ochester, General Editor